Q: Skills for Success 3
LISTENING AND SPEAKING

Teacher's Handbook

Susan Iannuzzi

OXFORD

UNIVERSITY PRESS

OXFORD
UNIVERSITY PRESS

198 Madison Avenue
New York, NY 10016 USA

Great Clarendon Street, Oxford ox2 6dp UK

Oxford University Press is a department of the University of Oxford.
It furthers the University's objective of excellence in research, scholarship,
and education by publishing worldwide in

Oxford New York

Auckland Cape Town Dar es Salaam Hong Kong Karachi
Kuala Lumpur Madrid Melbourne Mexico City Nairobi
New Delhi Shanghai Taipei Toronto

With offices in

Argentina Austria Brazil Chile Czech Republic France Greece
Guatemala Hungary Italy Japan Poland Portugal Singapore
South Korea Switzerland Thailand Turkey Ukraine Vietnam

General Manager, American ELT: Laura Pearson
Publisher: Stephanie Karras
Associate Publishing Manager: Sharon Sargent
Associate Development Editor: Keyana Shaw
Director, ADP: Susan Sanguily
Executive Design Manager: Maj-Britt Hagsted
Associate Design Manager: Michael Steinhofer
Electronic Production Manager: Julie Armstrong
Production Artist: Elissa Santos
Cover Design: Michael Steinhofer
Production Coordinator: Elizabeth Matsumoto

ISBN: 978-0-19-475617-4 Listening and Speaking 3 Teacher's Handbook Pack
ISBN: 978-0-19-475660-0 Listening and Speaking 3 Teacher's Handbook
ISBN: 978-0-19-475669-3 Reading & Writing/Listening & Speaking 3
                    Testing Program CD-ROM
ISBN: 978-0-19-475643-3 Q Online Practice Teacher Access Code Card

Printed in China

This book is printed on paper from certified and well-managed sources.

10 9 8 7 6

ACKNOWLEDGMENTS
*The publishers would like to thank the following for their kind permission to reproduce
photographs:*
p. vi Marcin Krygier/iStockphoto; xiii Rüstem GÜRLER/iStockphoto

CONTENTS

WELCOME TO Q:Skills for Success

Q: Skills for Success is a six-level series with two strands,
Reading and Writing and *Listening and Speaking*.

READING AND WRITING

LISTENING AND SPEAKING

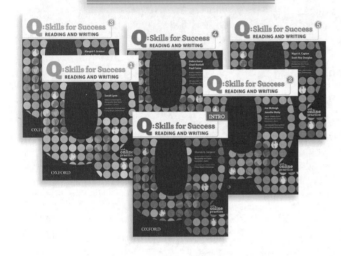

WITH Q ONLINE PRACTICE web

STUDENT AND TEACHER INFORMED

Q: Skills for Success is the result of an extensive development process involving thousands
of teachers and hundreds of students around the world. Their views and opinions helped
shape the content of the series. *Q* is grounded in teaching theory as well as real-world
classroom practice, making it the most learner-centered series available.

To the Teacher

Highlights of the *Q: Skills for Success* Teacher's Handbook

As you probably know from your own teaching experience, students want to know the point of a lesson. They want to know the "why" even when they understand the "how." In the classroom, the "why" is the learning outcome, and to be successful, students need to know it. The learning outcome provides a clear reason for classroom work and helps students meaningfully access new material.

Each unit in Oxford's *Q: Skills for Success* series builds around a thought-provoking question related to that unit's unique learning outcome. Students learn vocabulary to answer the unit question; consider new information related to the unit's theme that utilizes this vocabulary; use this information to think critically about new questions; and use those answers to practice the new listening, vocabulary, grammar, pronunciation, and speaking skills they need to achieve the unit's learning outcome.

Each aspect of the learning process in the Q series builds toward completing the learning outcome. This interconnected process of considering new information is at the heart of a critical thinking approach and forms the basis of the students' work in each unit of the Q series. At the end of the unit, students complete a practical project built around the learning outcome.

Learning outcomes create expectations in the classroom: expectations of what students will learn, what teachers will teach, and what lessons will focus on. Students benefit because they know they need to learn content for a purpose; teachers benefit because they can plan activities that reinforce the knowledge and skills students need to complete the learning outcome. In short, learning outcomes provide the focus that lessons need.

UNIT **6**

Unit QUESTION
Who makes you laugh?

Laughter

LISTENING • listening for specific information
VOCABULARY • synonyms
GRAMMAR • simple present for informal narratives
PRONUNCIATION • simple present third-person *-s/-es*
SPEAKING • using eye contact, pause, and tone of voice

LEARNING OUTCOME
Use appropriate eye contact, tone of voice, and pauses to tell a funny story or a joke to your classmates.

> In this example unit, students are asked to think about who makes them laugh while preparing to tell their own joke or funny story.

> The unit assignment ties into that unit's unique learning outcome.

Tell a Story or Joke	20 points	15 points	10 points	0 points
Student told the joke or funny story easily (without long pauses or reading) and was easy to understand (spoke clearly and at a good speed).				
Student used the simple present tense correctly.				
Student used vocabulary from the unit.				
Student used eye contact, pauses, and tone of voice to effectively tell the joke or funny story.				
Student correctly pronounced third person *-s/-es*.				

Total points: _____
Comments:

> Clear assessments allow both teachers and students to comment on and measure learner outcomes.

Q Unit Assignment: Tell a joke or a funny story

Unit Question (5 minutes)

Refer students back to the ideas they discussed at the beginning of the unit about who makes them laugh. Cue students if necessary by asking specific questions about the content of the unit: *Why did people think Jackie Chan was funny? What advice did we hear about how to be funny? What skills can you use to make your jokes and stories more entertaining?*

Learning Outcome

1. Tie the Unit Assignment to the unit learning outcome. Say: *The outcome for this unit is to use appropriate eye contact, tone of voice, and pauses to tell a funny story or a joke to your classmates. This Unit Assignment is going to let you show that you can do that as well as correctly use and pronounce the simple present.*

CRITICAL THINKING

A critical thinking approach asks students to process new information and to learn how to apply that information to a new situation. Teachers might set learning outcomes to give students targets to hit—for example: "After this lesson, give three reasons why people immigrate"—and the materials and exercises in the lesson provide students with the knowledge and skills to think critically and discover *their* three reasons.

Questions are important catalysts in the critical thinking process. Questions encourage students to reflect on and apply their knowledge to new situations. Students and teachers work together to understand, analyze, synthesize, and evaluate the lesson's questions and content to reach the stated outcomes. As students become more familiar with these stages of the critical thinking process, they will be able to use new information to complete tasks more efficiently and in unique and meaningful ways.

 **Tip** Critical Thinking

In Activity B, you have to **restate**, or say again in perhaps a different way, some of the information you learned in the two readings. **Restating** is a good way to review information.

Throughout the Student Book, *Critical Thinking Tips* accompany certain activities, helping students to practice and understand these critical thinking skills.

B (10 minutes)

1. Introduce the Unit Question, *Why do people immigrate to other countries?* Ask related information questions or questions about personal experience to help students prepare for answering the more abstract unit question: *Did you immigrate to this country? What were your reasons for leaving your home country? What were your reasons for choosing your new country? What did you bring with you?*

2. Tell students: *Let's start off our discussion by listing reasons why people might immigrate. For example, we could start our list with* finding work *because many people look for jobs in new countries. But there are many other reasons why people immigrate. What else can we think of?*

Critical Thinking Tip (1 minute)

1. Read the tip aloud.
2. Tell students that restating also helps to ensure that they have understood something correctly. After reading a new piece of information, they should try to restate it to a classmate who has also read the information, to ensure that they both have the same understanding of information.

The *Q Teacher's Handbook* features notes offering questions for expanded thought and discussion.

CRITICAL Q EXPANSION ACTIVITIES

The *Q Teacher's Handbook* expands on the critical thinking approach with the Critical Q Expansion Activities. These activities allow teachers to facilitate more practice for their students. The Critical Q Expansion Activities supplement the *Q Student Book* by expanding on skills and language students are practicing.

In today's classrooms, it's necessary that students have the ability to apply the skills they have learned to new situations with materials they have never seen before. *Q's* focus on critical thinking and the *Q Teacher's Handbook's* emphasis on practicing critical thinking skills through the Critical Q Expansion Activities prepares students to excel in this important skill.

The easy-to-use activity suggestions increase student practice and success with critical thinking skills.

Critical Q: Expansion Activity

Outlining

1. Explain to students: *A popular way to prepare to outline one's ideas is to use a cluster map. In a cluster map, a big circle is drawn in the middle of a page or on the board, and a main point is written inside it—**this will become the topic sentence in the outline.***

2. Then explain: *Next, lines are drawn away from the circle and new, smaller circles are attached to the other end of those lines. Inside each of the smaller circles, ideas are written which relate to the main point—**these become supporting sentences in the outline.***

21ST CENTURY SKILLS

Both the academic and professional worlds are becoming increasingly interdependent. The toughest problems are solved only when looked at from multiple perspectives. Success in the 21st century requires more than just core academic knowledge—though that is still crucial. Now, successful students have to collaborate, innovate, adapt, be self-directed, be flexible, be creative, be tech-literate, practice teamwork, and be accountable—both individually and in groups.

Q approaches language learning in light of these important 21st Century Skills. Each unit asks students to practice many of these attributes, from collaboration to innovation to accountability, *while* they are learning new language and content. The Q *Student Books* focus on these increasingly important skills with unique team, pair, and individual activities. Additionally, the Q *Teacher's Handbooks* provide support with easy-to-use 21st Century Skill sections for teachers who want to incorporate skills like "openness to other people's ideas and opinions" into their classrooms but aren't sure where to start.

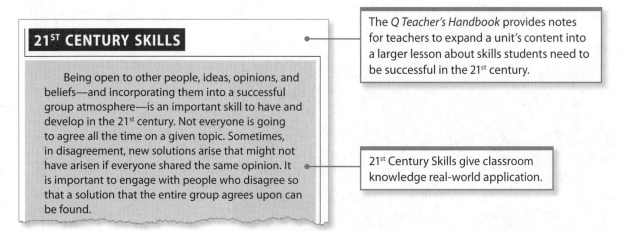

21ST CENTURY SKILLS

Being open to other people, ideas, opinions, and beliefs—and incorporating them into a successful group atmosphere—is an important skill to have and develop in the 21st century. Not everyone is going to agree all the time on a given topic. Sometimes, in disagreement, new solutions arise that might not have arisen if everyone shared the same opinion. It is important to engage with people who disagree so that a solution that the entire group agrees upon can be found.

The Q *Teacher's Handbook* provides notes for teachers to expand a unit's content into a larger lesson about skills students need to be successful in the 21st century.

21st Century Skills give classroom knowledge real-world application.

Q ONLINE PRACTICE

Q *Online Practice* is an online workbook that gives students quick access to all-new content in a range of additional practice activities. The interface is intuitive and user-friendly, allowing students to focus on enhancing their language skills.

For the teacher, Q *Online Practice* includes a digital grade book providing immediate and accurate assessment of each student's progress. Straightforward individual student or class reports can be viewed onscreen, printed, or exported, giving you comprehensive feedback on what students have mastered or where they need more help.

Teacher's Access Code Cards for the digital grade book are available upon adoption or for purchase. Use the access code to register for your Q *Online Practice* account at www.Qonlinepractice.com.

These features of the Q: *Skills for Success* series enable you to help your students develop the skills they need to succeed in their future academic and professional careers. By using learning outcomes, critical thinking, and 21st century skills, you help students gain a deeper knowledge of the material they are presented with, both in and out of the classroom.

Q connects critical thinking, language skills, and learning outcomes.

LANGUAGE SKILLS

Explicit skills instruction enables students to meet their academic and professional goals.

LEARNING OUTCOMES

Clearly identified **learning outcomes** focus students on the goal of their instruction.

UNIT **9**

Money

LISTENING	listening for signposts
VOCABULARY	using the dictionary
GRAMMAR	types of sentences
PRONUNCIATION	intonation in different types of sentences
SPEAKING	agreeing and disagreeing

LEARNING OUTCOME

Participate in a group discussion evaluating the influence money has on happiness.

Unit QUESTION

Can money buy happiness?

PREVIEW THE UNIT

A Discuss these questions with your classmates.

How much money do you think people really need to be happy? Explain.

Do you think more money would make you happier? Why or why not?

Look at the photo. Do you think the people living in this house are happy? Why or why not?

B Discuss the Unit Question above with your classmates.

Listen to *The Q Classroom*, Track 13 on CD 3, to hear other answers.

166 UNIT 9

167

CRITICAL THINKING

Thought-provoking **unit questions** engage students with the topic and provide a **critical thinking framework** for the unit.

 Having the learning outcome is important because it gives students and teachers a clear idea of what the point of each task/activity in the unit is.
Lawrence Lawson, Palomar College, California

PREVIEW LISTENING 1

LANGUAGE SKILLS

Two listening texts provide input on the unit question and give **exposure to academic content.**

Sudden Wealth

You are going to listen to a podcast that helps people learn to handle their money wisely. The article discusses people who suddenly become rich and the difficulties they face.

Which topics do you think the article will discuss? Check (✓) your ideas.

☐ how sudden wealth makes people happy

☐ how sudden wealth causes problems

☐ the advantages and disadvantages of sudden wealth

CRITICAL THINKING

Students **discuss** their opinions of each listening text and **analyze** how it changes their perspective on the unit question.

Q WHAT DO YOU THINK?

A. Discuss the questions in a group.

1. Which do you think comes first, happiness or money? Explain.

2. What qualities of a happy person do you think lead to better employment and financial outcomes?

Tip Critical Thinking

Question 1 of Activity B asks you to **choose** between two things. To make the best choice, you evaluate a variety of factors, including your knowledge and experience.

B. Think about both Listening 1 and Listening 2 as you discuss the questions.

1. What is the difference between sudden wealth and earning more money from a better job? Which would you prefer? Why?

2. Do you pay much attention to financial matters? Do you enjoy thinking about money, or does it make you feel stressed? Explain.

One of the best features is your focus on developing materials of a high "interest level."

Troy Hammond, Tokyo Gakugei University,
International Secondary School, Japan

Explicit skills instruction prepares students for academic success.

LANGUAGE SKILLS

Explicit instruction and practice in listening, speaking, grammar, pronunciation, and vocabulary skills **help students achieve language proficiency.**

LEARNING OUTCOMES

Practice activities allow students to **master the skills** before they are evaluated at the end of the unit.

Listening Skill | **Listening for signposts**

Signposts are words and phrases that can tell you the order in which things happened. Listen for signposts to help you follow the order of events and the logic in a text.

CD 3
Track 16

Listen to these examples of signposts from Listening 1.

First, it affects how our brains work, at least for a while.
In the beginning, when we get the money, our brain identifies it as pleasure.
Then that feeling wears off.

Here are some words and phrases which are used as signposts.

At the start	In the middle	At the end
At first,	After (that),	Finally,
First,	Before (that),	In conclusion,
In the beginning,	Later,	In summary,
	Next,	
	Second,	
	Then,	

CD 3
Track 17

A. Listen to a reporter interview a secretary who suddenly acquired a lot of money. Complete the interview with the signposts you hear.

Reporter: You are one of many people in this town who suddenly acquired a lot of wealth when your company was purchased by a large software company. How has that affected your life?

Laura Green: Well, _____ it was pretty incredible. It took a
                                    1
while for me to believe it. But _____ I began to realize what
                                              2
it could actually do to my life. Things have changed dramatically.

Reporter: In what way?

Laura: I paid off all of my credit card debt. And sent my son to college.
Receiving this money was just fantastic! _____, I was
                                                       3
worried all the time.

Reporter: So your financial circumstances have improved. What else has changed?

172   UNIT 9 | Can money buy happiness?

Speaking Skill | **Agreeing and disagreeing**

There are certain phrases used for **agreeing and disagreeing**. It's important to know which phrases and expressions are appropriate for formal and informal situations. An informal conversation is very different from a formal discussion at college or at work.

Here are some phrases you can use when you want to agree or disagree in different situations.

Agreeing		Disagreeing
I agree (completely).	formal	I disagree.
That's exactly what I think.		I don't agree (at all).
That's a good point.		Sorry, but that's not my opinion.
That's right.		I don't feel the same way.
I think so too.		I don't think so.
Absolutely!		No way!
Yeah, I know!	informal	Oh, come on!

CD 3
Track 22

A. Listen to the conversations. Complete each conversation with the phrases you hear.

Ellie: What are you going to do with the money your grandfather gave you?

Sam: I'm not sure. I think I'm going to take an expensive vacation.

Ellie: Really? Don't you have a lot of school loans to pay?

Sam: _____. Maybe the vacation's not such a good idea.
              1

Ellie: _____. Vacations are fun, but it's much more important
              2
to pay off your debt.

Monica: I think raising the average income in countries around the world is the best way to increase the level of happiness.

Patricia: I _____. More money might make the very poor
                 3
happier, but not everyone.

Monica: I _____. I think everyone except perhaps the very
                 4
wealthy will benefit from a higher income.

Patricia: Well, I can see we'll just have to agree to disagree.

182   UNIT 9 | Can money buy happiness?

The tasks are simple, accessible, user-friendly, and very useful.
Jessica March, American University of Sharjah, U.A.E.

Vocabulary Skill | **Using the dictionary** web+

Definitions of similar words

Some words are similar in meaning, for instance, *creativity* and *productivity*.

> People in jobs where they can show creativity and productivity are happier than those who aren't.

Creativity and *productivity* both have to do with making things, but they are also a little different. Look at their dictionary definitions.

> **cre·a·tiv·i·ty** AWL /ˌkrieɪˈtɪvəti/ *noun* [U] the ability to make or produce new things, especially using skill or imagination: *teaching that encourages children's creativity*

> **pro·duc·tiv·i·ty** /ˌprɑdʌkˈtɪvəti; ˌproʊ-/ *noun* [U] the rate at which a worker, a company, or a country produces goods, and the amount produced: *More efficient methods will lead to greater productivity.*

All dictionary entries are taken from the *Oxford American Dictionary for learners of English.*

LEARNER CENTERED

Q Online Practice provides all new content for additional practice in an easy-to-use online workbook. Every student book includes a ***Q Online Practice access code card.*** Use the access code to register for your *Q Online Practice* account at www.Qonlinepractice.com.

LANGUAGE SKILLS

A **research-based vocabulary program** focuses students on the words they need to know academically and professionally, using skill strategies based on the same research as the Oxford dictionaries.

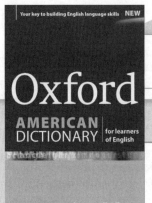

Your key to building English language skills **NEW**

Oxford

AMERICAN DICTIONARY for learners of English

Improve your writing with Oxford **iWriter**

All dictionary entries are taken from the *Oxford American Dictionary for learners of English.*

The ***Oxford American Dictionary for learners of English*** was developed with English learners in mind, and provides extra learning tools for pronunciation, verb types, basic grammar structures, and more.

The Oxford 3000™ 🔑

The Oxford 3000 encompasses **the 3000 most important words to learn in English**. It is based on a comprehensive analysis of the Oxford English Corpus, a two-billion word collection of English text, and on extensive research with both language and pedagogical experts.

The Academic Word List AWL

The Academic Word List was created by Averil Coxhead and contains **570 words that are commonly used in academic English**, such as in textbooks or articles across a wide range of academic subject areas. These words are a great place to start if you are studying English for academic purposes.

Clear learning outcomes focus students on the goals of instruction.

Unit Assignment | **Take part in a group discussion**

 In this assignment, you are going to take part in a group discussion about money and happiness. As you prepare for the discussion, think about the Unit Question, "Can money buy happiness?" and refer to the Self-Assessment checklist on page 184.

For alternative unit assignments, see the *Q: Skills for Success Teacher's Handbook.*

CONSIDER THE IDEAS

Work with a partner. Discuss the questions about money and happiness. Be sure to use the correct intonation when you ask each other questions.

What is money's influence on happiness?

What kind of person do you think would be happier with more money? Why?

Would your life be different if you had more or less money? How?

Is it more enjoyable to give or receive money? Why?

182   **UNIT 9** | Can money buy happiness?

Check (✓) the skills you learned. If you need more work on a skill, refer to the page(s) in parentheses.

LISTENING	I can listen for signposts. (p. 172)
VOCABULARY	I can use the dictionary to find the definition of similar words. (p. 178)
GRAMMAR	I can use different types of sentences. (p. 180)
PRONUNCIATION	I can use correct intonation in different sentence types. (p. 181)
SPEAKING	I can use phrases for agreeing and disagreeing. (p. 181)
LEARNING OUTCOME	I can participate in a group discussion evaluating the influence money has on happiness.

| Listening and Speaking   **185**

 Students can check their learning ... and they can focus on the essential points when they study.

Suh Yoomi, Seoul, South Korea

Q Online Practice

For the student

- **Easy-to-use:** a simple interface allows students to focus on enhancing their speaking and listening skills, not learning a new software program
- **Flexible:** for use anywhere there's an Internet connection
- **Access code card:** a *Q Online Practice* access code is included with the student book. Use the access code to register for *Q Online Practice* at www.Qonlinepractice.com

For the teacher

- **Simple yet powerful:** automatically grades student exercises and tracks progress
- **Straightforward:** online management system to review, print, or export reports
- **Flexible:** for use in the classroom or easily assigned as homework
- **Access code card:** contact your sales rep for your *Q Online Practice* teacher's access code

Teacher Resources

Q Teacher's Handbook gives strategic support through:

- specific teaching notes for each activity
- ideas for ensuring student participation
- multilevel strategies and expansion activities
- the answer key
- special sections on 21st century skills and critical thinking
- a *Testing Program CD-ROM* with a customizable test for each unit.

For additional resources visit the *Q: Skills for Success* companion website at www.oup.com/elt/teacher/Qskillsforsuccess

Q Class Audio includes:

- listening texts
- pronunciation presentations and exercises
- *The Q Classroom*

> " It's an interesting, engaging series which provides plenty of materials that are easy to use in class, as well as instructionally promising. "
> *Donald Weasenforth, Collin College, Texas*

UNIT	LISTENING	SPEAKING	VOCABULARY
1 First Impressions Q **Are first impressions accurate?** **LISTENING 1:** The Psychology of First Impressions A lecture (Psychology) **LISTENING 2:** Book Review of *Blink* by Malcolm Gladwell A radio program (Interpersonal Communication)	• Use prior knowledge and personal experience to predict content • Listen for main ideas • Listen for details • Make inferences to fully understand what a speaker means • Listen for opinions to understand a book review • Listen for reduced verb forms to understand everyday speech	• Make notes to prepare for a presentation or group discussion • Take turns to make a conversation go smoothly • Imply opinions to avoid stating them too directly • Use verb contractions to increase naturalness of speech	• Assess your prior knowledge of vocabulary • Use suffixes to change a word's part of speech
2 Food and Taste Q **What's more important: taste or nutrition?** **LISTENING 1:** You Are What You Eat A radio program (Nutrition) **LISTENING 2:** Food Tasters A podcast (Food Service)	• Use prior knowledge and personal experience to predict content • Listen for main ideas • Listen for details • Listen for causes and effects to understand relationships among ideas • Follow a summary of several ideas to match an opinion with a speaker • Identify /j/ and /w/ sounds in speech to understand links between words	• Make notes to prepare for an interview • Give advice to suggest healthy eating habits • Prepare to speak about your personal tastes to help others conduct a survey • Conduct a survey of classmates' tastes • Participate in a group discussion about results of a survey	• Assess your prior knowledge of vocabulary • Understand and use collocations of adjectives with nouns to expand vocabulary
3 Success Q **What can we learn from success and failure?** **LISTENING 1:** Chasing Your Dreams A lecture (Business Management) **LISTENING 2:** The Benefits of Failure A speech (Psychology)	• Use prior knowledge and personal experience to predict content • Listen for main ideas • Listen for details • Listen for opinion statements to understand a speaker's positive and negative attitudes • Match people with ideas to understand their attitudes • Listen for exact words or phrases to improve your word recognition	• Make notes to prepare for a presentation or group discussion • Ask for clarification so you understand difficult concepts • Include time for questions after a presentation so your audience can ask for clarification • Clarify what you say so others understand you better	• Assess your prior knowledge of vocabulary • Understand and use prefixes for negatives (*dis-*, *im-*, and *ir-*) and other meanings (*co-*, *re-*, *multi-*, and *anti-*) • Understand prefixes to increase comprehension • Use prefixes to expand vocabulary

GRAMMAR	PRONUNCIATION	CRITICAL THINKING	UNIT OUTCOME
• Auxiliary verbs *do, be, have*	• Use contractions with auxiliary verbs	• Assess your prior knowledge of content • Relate personal experiences to listening topics • Integrate information from multiple sources • Evaluate the truthfulness of traditional wisdom • Identify your decision-making processes • Examine your reasons for forming impressions of people	• Describe in detail an inaccurate first impression.
• Quantifiers with count/ non-count nouns	• Use linked sounds with /j/ and /w/	• Assess your prior knowledge of content • Relate personal experiences to listening topics • Integrate information from multiple sources • Identify personal tastes in food • Evaluate the healthfulness of your habits • Relate personal food preferences to those of your classmates • Evaluate classmates' reasons for food preferences	• Interview classmates to inform a group discussion on why people prefer certain foods.
• Gerunds and infinitives as the objects of verbs	• Correctly place stress on important words in sentences.	• Assess your prior knowledge of content • Relate personal experiences to listening topics • Integrate information from multiple sources • Understand, interpret, and evaluate others' attitudes toward succes and failure • Identify your attitudes toward success and failure • Consider your hopes and ambitions • Evaluate the consequences of decisions	• Discuss successful and unsuccessful personal experiences and explain what you learned from them.

UNIT	LISTENING	SPEAKING	VOCABULARY
4 New Perspectives **Q** **Is change good or bad?** **LISTENING 1:** Changing Expectations A talk (Finance) **LISTENING 2:** An Interview with Barbara Ehrenreich An interview (Journalism, Sociology)	• Use prior knowledge and personal experience to predict content • Listen for main ideas • Listen for details • Listen to personal stories to understand other people's experiences • Use a T-chart to take effective notes • Listen for intonation to identify a speaker's level of interest in a topic • Listen for exact words or phrases to improve your word recognition	• Make notes to prepare for a presentation or group discussion • Describe a situation using details so a listener can make inferences about an event • Ask for reasons to understand why something happened • Express reasons to explain why something happened • Use reasons to explain personal beliefs	• Assess your prior knowledge of vocabulary • Understand dictionary entries to diagram meanings in word webs
5 Responsibility **Q** **Are we responsible for the world we live in?** **LISTENING 1:** Corporate Social Responsibility A lecture (Business, Ecology) **LISTENING 2:** Personal Responsibility An excerpt from a college seminar (Business, Sociology)	• Use prior knowledge and personal experience to predict content • Listen for main ideas • Listen for details • Listen for supporting statements to apply a general concept to real life • Use intonation, volume, and other features to infer a speaker's attitudes • Listen for exact words in a conversation to improve your word recognition	• Take notes to prepare for a presentation or group discussion • Practice varying intonation and other features to convey your attitudes • Add tag questions to statements to find out what someone thinks • Answer tag questions using proper grammar and intonation to accurately express what you think • Lead a discussion so it proceeds smoothly, fairly, and stays on topic	• Assess your prior knowledge of vocabulary • Find the most relevant dictionary definition for a word that has many meanings
6 Advertising **Q** **How can advertisers change our behavior?** **LISTENING 1:** Advertising Techniques A small group presentation (Advertising) **LISTENING 2:** Advertising Ethics and Standards An interview (Business, Ethics)	• Use prior knowledge and personal experience to predict content • Listen for main ideas • Listen for details • Listen for evidence to distinguish fact from opinion • Listen for modal verbs to understand obligations, prohibitions, and recommendations • Listen for intonation to distinguish between statements and questions • Listen for exact words or phrases to improve your word recognition	• Make notes to prepare for a presentation or group discussion • Use modals to express obligation, prohibition, and recommendation • Ask questions and make statements with correct intonation to be understood clearly • Give reasons and examples to support opinions you express	• Assess your prior knowledge of vocabulary • Use context to understand the meanings of unfamiliar words or phrases

GRAMMAR	PRONUNCIATION	CRITICAL THINKING	UNIT OUTCOME
• Simple past and present perfect	• Vary intonation to show interest in a topic	• Assess your prior knowledge of content • Relate personal experiences to listening topics • Integrate information from multiple sources • Recall life experiences and assess their significance • Consider the methods used by reporters to gather information	• Participate in a group discussion emphasizing the advantages and disadvantages of change.
• Tag questions	• Use rising and falling intonation in tag questions to convey meaning	• Assess your prior knowledge of content • Relate personal experiences to listening topics • Integrate information from multiple sources • Consider social responsibility on several levels, including individual, family, and corporate responsibility • Develop skills for leadership in a small group	• State and explain your opinions about our responsibility for issues impacting our world.
• Modals that express attitude	• Correctly use intonation in *yes/no* and *wh-* questions • Use intonation to make statements into questions to express surprise	• Assess your prior knowledge of content • Relate personal experiences to listening topics • Integrate information from multiple sources • Assess your personal experiences with advertising and your responses to it • Judge real-life situations according to your ethical standards • Summarize a discussion in a group • Express and support a personal opinion	• State and support your opinions concerning the influence of advertising on our behavior.

UNIT	LISTENING	SPEAKING	VOCABULARY
7 Risk **What risks are good to take?** **LISTENING 1: Financing a Dream** A talk (Finance, Film Study) **LISTENING 2: The Truth about the Loch Ness Monster** A report (Zoology)	• Use prior knowledge and personal experience to predict content • Listen for main ideas • Listen for details • Listen for numbers to correctly understand amounts • Use the form of number expressions to distinguish between cardinal and ordinal numbers • Listen for exact words in a passage to improve your word recognition	• Make notes to prepare for a presentation or group discussion • Clearly introduce the topic of a presentation to focus an audience's attention • Use sequence expressions to clarify the order of events in a presentation • Use expressions of purpose/reason to explain actions and attitudes	• Assess your prior knowledge of vocabulary • Use a dictionary to learn about word families • Increase vocabulary by understanding word families
8 Cities **What do our cities say about us?** **LISTENING 1: Do cities have personalities?** A report (Urban studies) **LISTENING 2: Buenos Aires, Beijing, and Dubai** A description from 3 writers (Sociology)	• Use prior knowledge and personal experience to predict content • Listen for main ideas • Listen for details • Understand figurative expressions to interpret a speaker's true meaning • Listen for comments that help you match a city to a description	• Make notes to prepare for a presentation or group discussion • Use summary or recap techniques to end a presentation • Use a T-chart to take notes for a presentation	• Assess your prior knowledge of vocabulary • Understand phrasal verbs to accurately interpret statements
9 Money **Can money buy happiness?** **LISTENING 1: Sudden Wealth** A podcast (Psychology) **LISTENING 2: Happiness Breeds Success…and Money!** An interview (Personal finance, Psychology)	• Use prior knowledge and personal experience to predict content • Listen for main ideas • Listen for details • Listen for a sequence of factors to understand the stages in a process • Understand examples to relate them to larger ideas • Listen for signposts to understand the structure of a passage • Listen for exact words in a conversation to improve your word recognition	• Make notes to prepare for a presentation or group discussion • Use expressions to introduce statements of agreement and disagreement • Explain reasons to justify statements about personal preferences • Discuss with a partner attitudes about the relationship between money and happiness	• Assess your prior knowledge of vocabulary • Use a dictionary to distinguish among words that are somewhat similar in meaning
10 Keeping in Touch **Do we need technology to communicate long distance** **LISTENING 1: An Unusual Language** A lecture (Communication) **LISTENING 2: Message in a Bottle** A report (Sociology)	• Use prior knowledge and personal experience to predict content • Listen for main ideas • Listen for details • Listening for rhetorical questions to understand the structure of a lecture • Recognize definitions in a passage to understand unfamiliar vocabulary • Listen for exact words in sentences to improve your word recognition	• Take notes to prepare for a presentation or group discussion • Ask questions to confirm your understanding of definitions • Practice using idioms to increase the naturalness of your speech • Use adjectives, fixed phrases, and idioms to express emotions • Prepare a dialogue with a partner to improve your conversation skills	• Assess your prior knowledge of vocabulary • Understand idioms to accurately interpret statements • Correctly use idiomatic expressions

GRAMMAR	PRONUNCIATION	CRITICAL THINKING	UNIT OUTCOME
• Past perfect	• Correctly use contracted and uncontracted forms of *had*	• Assess your prior knowledge of content • Relate personal experiences to listening topics • Integrate information from multiple sources • Evaluate risks to determine which are justified • Reflect on your own willingness to take risks • Explain and evaluate a risk you have taken	• Give a short presentation on a risk you have taken, explaining your reasons for taking that risk.
• Separable and inseparable phrasal verbs	• Effectively link consonants and vowels	• Assess your prior knowledge of content • Relate personal experiences to listening topics • Integrate information from multiple sources • Evaluate the strengths and weaknesses of several entities • Classify items according to shared features • Assess the significance of an item's characteristics • Analyze personal preferences	• Give and recap a presentation highlighting what you like and dislike about a particular city.
• Sentence types—declarative, interrogatory, imperative, and exclamatory	• Effectively use intonation in different sentence types	• Assess your prior knowledge of content • Relate personal experiences to listening topics • Integrate information from multiple sources • Examine your attitudes toward money and happiness • Distinguish between causal relationships and correlations in research results • Support opinions with reasons an examples	• Participate in a group discussion evaluating the influence money has on happiness.
• Comparatives with adjectives	• Correctly pronounce unstressed connecting words	• Assess your prior knowledge of content • Relate personal experiences to listening topics • Integrate information from multiple sources • Reflect on personal styles of communication • Speculate about the origins of communication practices • Evaluate the effect of technology on language and communication • Decide how to resolve communication problems	• Role-play a phone call discussing an emotional event you have experienced.

Unit QUESTION

Are first impressions accurate?

First Impressions

LISTENING • making inferences
VOCABULARY • suffixes
GRAMMAR • auxiliary verbs *do, be, have*
PRONUNCIATION • contractions with auxiliary verbs
SPEAKING • taking coversational turns

LEARNING OUTCOME

Describe an inaccurate first
impression in detail.

▶ *Listening and Speaking 3, pages 2–3*

Preview the Unit

Learning Outcome

1. Ask for a volunteer to read the unit skills and then the unit learning outcome.

2. Explain: *The learning outcome is what you are expected to be able to do by the unit's end. You are going to be evaluated on how well you meet this outcome. With this in mind, you should focus on learning skills (Listening, Vocabulary, Grammar, Pronunciation, Speaking) that will support your goal of describing an inaccurate first impression in detail. This can also help you act as mentors in the classroom to help the other students meet this outcome.*

A (15 minutes)

1. Prepare students for thinking about the topic by eliciting the meaning of *first impression*. Then tell them about your first impression of someone you recently met. Explain where you met the person and why you had this impression of them.

2. Put students in pairs or small groups to discuss the first two questions.

3. Call on volunteers to share their ideas with the class. Ask questions to facilitate the discussion: *Did you notice physical characteristics more than other things? How much influence did the person's clothing have on your opinion? Did the place in which you met the person influence your opinion? Why or why not? Did the person speak to you directly? Did this influence your opinion of the person?*

4. Focus students' attention on the photo. Have a volunteer describe the photo to the class. Read the third question aloud. Ask additional questions: *Do you think these people know each other? Why?*

Activity A Answers, p. 3
Possible answers:

1. Students may mention physical appearance, clothing, or voice as things they first notice.

2. Students may think first impressions are important because they may not have the opportunity to correct a negative first impression. Some students may think first impressions are not important because a person's true character will be revealed eventually.

3. They could be meeting a friend or relative for the first time.

B (15 minutes)

1. Explain that each unit in Q focuses on a Unit Question that students will consider throughout the unit and will address in their Unit Assignment at the end of the unit.

2. Introduce the Unit Question, "Are first impressions accurate?" Ask related information questions or questions about personal experience to help students prepare for answering the unit question, which is more abstract. *Have you ever had a negative first impression about someone that you found was inaccurate or accurate? What happened to support or disprove your first impression?*

3. Give students a minute to silently consider their answers to the Unit Question. Then ask students whose answer is yes to stand on one side of the room and students whose answer is no to stand on the other side of the room.

4. Direct students to tell a partner next to them their reasons for choosing that side of the issue.

5. Call on volunteers from each side to share their opinions with the class.

6. After students have shared their opinions, provide an opportunity for anyone who would like to change sides to do so.

7. Ask students to sit down, copy the Unit Question and make a note of their answer and their reasons. They will refer to these notes at the end of the unit.

Activity B Answers, p. 3
Possible answers: First impressions may or may not be accurate. The accuracy of a first impression is revealed over time; Sometimes first impressions are accurate and sometimes they are not. We don't know unless we know the person for a long time; Maybe or maybe not. We need time to see.

The Q Classroom
 CD1, Track 2

1. Play *The Q Classroom.* Use the example from the audio to help students continue the conversation. Ask: *How did the students answer the question? Do you agree or disagree with their ideas? Why?*

2. On the audio, the students give examples of behavior that gives a good impression (smiling, being friendly) and those that give a bad first impression (being in a bad mood). Explore this idea further by eliciting other ways in which someone can make a good or bad impression (they like / don't like the same things you like, they are / aren't helpful, etc.)

▶ *Listening and Speaking 3, page 4*

C (10 minutes)

1. Direct students to read the instructions. Explain that they should say whether each proverb means that first impressions are accurate or not accurate.

2. Put students in pairs to discuss their answers.

3. Elicit answers and ask students to support them, e.g., *Don't judge a horse by its saddle* is accurate because a good horse can have a bad saddle, etc.

Activity C Answers, p. 4
1. N; **2.** N; **3.** A; **4.** N; **5.** N; **6.** A; **7.** A; **8.** N

MULTILEVEL OPTION
Allow lower-level students to match the proverbs and the pictures. Encourage higher-level students to create their own proverbs using those in the exercise as models, e.g., If it barks like a dog, it's a dog.

D (5 minutes)

1. If possible, place students in pairs from different cultures. Ask them to share proverbs about first impressions from their cultures.

2. If your students are from the same cultural background, you can elicit answers from the class.

E (10 minutes)

1. Keep or put students in pairs to discuss their opinions about the proverbs in Activity C.

2. Ask each student to report to the class which proverb their partner thinks is truest and why.

LISTENING

▶ *Listening and Speaking 3, page 5*

LISTENING 1:
The Psychology of First Impressions

VOCABULARY (15 minutes)

1. Direct students to read the words and their definitions. Elicit any difficulties or questions.

2. Ask students to complete the sentences.

3. Put students in pairs to check their answers.

4. Ask volunteers to read their answers. Elicit or provide corrections as necessary.

MULTILEVEL OPTION
Group lower-level students and assist them with the task. Point out the cues in the sentences that will help them to choose the correct word.
After higher-level students have checked answers in pairs, tell the pairs to write an additional sentence using the new word. Have volunteers write their sentence on the board. Correct the sentences with the whole class, focusing on the use of vocabulary word rather than other grammatical issues.

Vocabulary Answers, p. 5
1. sample;   **2.** errors;   **3.** assume;   **4.** briefly;
5. behavior;   **6.** form an impression;   **7.** negative;
8. trait;   **9.** positive;   **10.** encounter

For additional practice with the vocabulary, have students visit *Q Online Practice.*

▶ *Listening and Speaking 3, page 6*
PREVIEW LISTENING 1 (10 minutes)

1. Direct students to look at the photo. Help students to explore their own process for making first impressions. Ask: *What is your first impression of*

this woman? Help students to identify the factors that influenced their impression, for example, gender, dress, and facial expression.

2. Read the introductory paragraph and the answer choices aloud. Have students check their answers. Tell students they should review their answers after listening.

> **Preview Listening 1 Answers, p. 6**
> Students' answers will vary.

Listening 1 Background Note

Remind students that it's important to make a good first impression, especially in job interviews. Psychological research shows that when evaluating people, we weigh initial information more heavily than later information. The first information we get about a person influences the way we perceive subsequent information. As a result, we are more likely to believe that the first things we learn about someone are true.

For example, if you show an interest in people during a first meeting, they may form an impression of you as an engaging and caring person. They might not notice or care if you are distracted or selfish later.

Conversely, a negative first impression makes an even deeper impact. If you initially appear distracted or selfish, people may ignore your later caring behavior or interest toward them. It can take many additional positive actions to overcome the impact of a negative first impression.

LISTEN FOR MAIN IDEAS (5 minutes)

CD1, Track 3

1. Ask students to read the statements. Elicit any questions about them.
2. Play the audio and have students complete the activity individually.
3. Elicit the answers from the class.

> **Main Idea Answers, p. 6**
> **1.** F; **2.** T; **3.** F; **4.** T

LISTEN FOR DETAILS (10 minutes)

CD1, Track 4

1. Direct students to read the sentences before they listen again. Elicit any questions about them.
2. As you play the audio, have students listen and choose the correct answer.

3. Have students compare answers with a partner.
4. Replay the audio so that the partners can check their answers.
5. Go over the answers with the class.

> **Listen for Details Answers, p. 6**
> **1.** a; **2.** c; **3.** a; **4.** a; **5.** b

 For additional practice with listening comprehension, have students visit *Q Online Practice*.

Tip for Success (1 minute)

1. Read the tip aloud.
2. Elicit the anecdote used in Listening 1 (the coffee shop incident).
3. Ask students if they found this anecdote to be an interesting way to introduce the topic. Ask them to give reasons.

▶ *Listening and Speaking 3, page 7*

WHAT DO YOU THINK? (10 minutes)

1. Ask students to read the questions and reflect on their answers.
2. Seat students in small groups and assign roles: a group leader to make sure everyone contributes, a note-taker to record the group's ideas, a reporter to share the group's ideas with the class, and a timekeeper to watch the clock.
3. Give students five minutes to discuss the questions. Call time if conversations are winding down. Allow them an extra minute or two if necessary.
4. Call on each group's reporter to share ideas with the class.

> **What Do You Think? Answers, p. 7**
> Answers will vary. Possible answers:
> **1.** Yes, have met people who were very friendly when I first met them, and they still are.; No, sometimes people may be nervous when meeting someone for the first time and behave differently than they usually do.
> **2.** Yes, I know someone who was quiet and unfriendly when I first met her. After I got to know her, I realized that she is just very shy.

Learning Outcome

Use the Learning Outcome to frame the purpose and relevance of Listening 1. Ask: *What did you learn from Listening 1 that preprares you to describe an inaccurate first impression? What did you learn that will help you understand your own behavior when making first impressions?*

▶ *Listening and Speaking 3, page 8*

Listening Skill: Making inferences
(10 minutes)

 CD1, Track 5

1. Ask students to read the information about making inferences. Elicit any difficulties or questions.

2. Tell students they are going to listen to a student talking about his first meeting with his professor. Ask them to read along while they listen and underline the positive or negative things the student says about the meeting.

3. Read the text below the description of the meeting. Ask: *Did the student say anything negative about the meeting? What positive things did the student say? Did your answers match those listed in the book?*

A (5 minutes)
 CD1, Track 6

1. Ask students to read the questions before they listen. Elicit any questions about what students are instructed to do.

2. Play the audio while students take notes in their notebooks.

3. Tell students to write their answers to the questions. Do not elicit answers until students have completed Activity B.

B (5 minutes)

1. Put students in pairs to compare their answers.

2. Elicit answers to the questions from Activity A.

> **Listening Skill Answers, p. 8**
> **1.** It was a positive first impression. Supporting information may include: Lee smiled; He had a firm handshake; He was helpful.
> **2.** Yes, the speaker likes Lee. Supporting information may include: The speaker hoped to see him again; When she did, she invited Lee to join her lunch table.

C (5 minutes)
 CD1, Track 7

1. Keep students in pairs. Tell them they are going to listen to the speaker's opinion about Lee. Tell them to take notes in their notebook and explain that they will compare them to the notes that they took in Activity A.

2. Play the audio while students take notes.

3. Tell students to compare these notes with those from Activity A.

4. Call on several pairs to share their answers.

D (5 minutes)

1. Keep students in pairs. Read the directions aloud to the class.

2. Tell partners to describe meeting someone for the first time. Students should make inferences about their partner's opinions.

3. Call on several pairs to report their partner's inferences to the class and say whether they were correct or not and why.

 For additional practice with making inferences, have students visit *Q Online Practice*.

▶ *Listening and Speaking 3, page 9*

LISTENING 2: Book Review of *Blink* by Malcolm Gladwell

VOCABULARY (10 minutes)

1. Ask students to locate the bold words in each sentence. Pronounce and have students repeat the words.

2. Have students read the sentences and circle the correct answer for each. Call on volunteers to read the answers aloud.

> **Vocabulary Answers, p. 9**
> **1.** b; **2.** a; **3.** c; **4.** a; **5.** a;
> **6.** a; **7.** c; **8.** c; **9.** b; **10.** a

 For additional practice with the vocabulary, have students visit *Q Online Practice*.

▶ *Listening and Speaking 3, page 10*

PREVIEW LISTENING 2 (5 minutes)

1. Direct students to read the information. Ask: *Why do you think Malcolm Gladwell used the title* Blink *for a book about making decisions based on first impressions?* Explain that the title comes from the expression "in the blink of an eye," which means extremely quickly.

2. Ask students to check the things they think they could easily make a quick decision about. Point out they can check more than one or none of the things. Tell them to look back at their answers after they listen to see if they still agree with their choices.

Listening 2 Background Note

Malcolm Gladwell is a writer for the magazine *The New Yorker*. He has also written several best-selling non-fiction books, including *The Tipping Point* and *Outliers*. His books describe various phenomena within the fields of psychology and social psychology, including popularity trends and the factors that contribute to success.

His book *Blink* was published in 2005 and examines the way in which people unconsciously process information to make an accurate first impression. Gladwell is of British and Jamaican ancestry, but was raised in Canada. He now lives in New York.

LISTEN FOR MAIN IDEAS (5 minutes)

CD1, Track 8

1. Direct students to read the sentences and answer choices. Tell them they will choose one answer for each sentence.
2. Play the audio and have students complete the activity individually.
3. Call on volunteers for the answers.

> **Listen for Main Ideas Answers, p. 10**
> **1.** b;   **2.** b;   **3.** b;   **4.** c

▶ *Listening and Speaking 3, page 11*

LISTEN FOR DETAILS (10 minutes)

CD1, Track 9

1. Explain that students are going to match a detail about the listening with the example given in the review.
2. Direct students to read the details and examples.
3. As you play the audio, have students match the details and examples individually.
4. Have students compare answers with a partner.
5. Go over the answers with the class.

> **Listen for Details Answers, p. 11**
> **1.** e;   **2.** d;   **3.** b;   **4.** c;   **5.** a

 For additional practice with listening comprehension, have students visit *Q Online Practice*.

WHAT DO YOU THINK?

A (10 minutes)

1. Ask students to read the questions and reflect on their answers.

2. Seat students in small groups and assign roles: a group leader to make sure everyone contributes, a note-taker to record the group's ideas, a reporter to share the group's ideas with the class, and a timekeeper to watch the clock.

3. Give students five minutes to discuss the questions. Call time if conversations are winding down. Allow them an extra minute or two if necessary.

4. Call on each group's reporter to share ideas with the class.

> **Activity A Answers, p. 11**
> Answers will vary. Possible answers:
> **1.** Yes, I think it's best to trust your instinct for difficult decisions; No, there are some difficult decisions that require a lot of thought, such as taking a new job.
> **2.** Yes, I think our first impression provide us with accurate information; No, I think that first impressions can be misleading.

Tip for Critical Thinking (1 minute)

1. Read the tip aloud.
2. Point out that comparing and contrasting is an essential skill for making decisions in academic and professional settings.
3. Explain that sometimes we may focus on similarities more than differences, or vice-versa. Remind students that it is important to consider both.

Critical Q: Expansion Activity

Comparing and contrasting

1. Present students with two extremely different things, for example, a magazine photo of an actor, athlete, singer, or celebrity in an ad and one of a person selling a household cleaning product.
2. Ask students to compare and contrast the photos. Point out that they should compare and contrast on a variety of levels, including objective characteristics such as gender or age, as well as subjective characteristics such as trustworthiness or approachability.
3. Give students a time limit, such as 5 minutes, to compare and contrast.
4. Put students in small groups to share their opinions. Ask each group to choose a reporter.
5. Call on reporters to share their group's findings.

B (5 minutes)

1. Have students continue working in their small groups to discuss the questions in Activity B. Tell

them to choose a new leader, recorder, reporter, and timekeeper.

2. Call on the new reporter to share the group's answers to the questions.

Activity B Answers, p. 11
Answers will vary. Possible answers:
1. Students may support their opinions based on the general success or failure of their first impressions in the past.
2. Students may suggest that stressful situations often lead to accurate first impressions because people show their real character.

Learning Outcome

Use the learning outcome to frame the purpose and relevance of Listenings 1 and 2 and the Critical Q activity of comparing and contrasting. Ask: *What did you learn from comparing and contrasting that prepares you to describe a first impression? What did you learn that will help you to select or recall details about why you made that first impression?*

▶ *Listening and Speaking 3, page 12*

Vocabulary Skill: Suffixes (10 minutes)

1. Direct students to read the information silently.

2. Read the words aloud to model correct stress and pronunciation. Ask students to repeat them.

3. Check comprehension: *What do these words mean? What base word is this noun, verb, adjective, or adverb from? Does the noun refer to a person or an abstraction?*

Skill Note

Point out that suffixes appear at the end of many words and that students can determine the part of speech of a new or unknown word by thinking about other words they know that have the same suffix. For example, if students know that *amusement* is a noun because it ends in *–ment*, they can determine that *entertainment* is also a noun.

Explain that the suffixes may give more information than the part of speech. For example, the noun suffixes *-er* and *-or* refer to people, e.g., *writer, manager, director, actor,* etc. Similarly, the suffix *-ness* can turn an adjective into a noun, e.g. *sad* → *sadness* and *happy* → *happiness.*

A (15 minutes)

1. Direct students not to use their dictionaries for this exercise. Tell them to use the example words from the skill box for help.

2. Go over the answers with the class.

Activity A Answers, p. 12

New word	Suffix	Part of speech	Base word
2. assumption	-(p)tion	noun	assume
3. consciously	-ly	adverb	conscious
4. prediction	-(t)ion	noun	predict
5. effectively	-ly	adverb	effective
6. instinctive	-ive	adjective	instinct
7. selection	-(t)ion	noun	select

B (10 minutes)

1. Put students in pairs to discuss the meanings of the new words.

2. Tell students to use their dictionaries to check any meanings they are unsure of. Go over the answers as a class.

Activity B Answers, p. 12
Read the dictionary definitions aloud and discuss any uncertainties or questions.

MULTILEVEL OPTION

Group lower-level students and assist them with the task. Help them find the words in the dictionary and check their meanings.

After higher-level students have confirmed meanings in pairs, tell the pairs to write sentences using the new word. Have volunteers write their sentences on the board. Correct the sentences with the whole class, focusing on the meaning of the word as well as correct part of speech.

▶ *Listening and Speaking 3, page 13*

C (10 minutes)

1. Ask pairs to complete the sentences using words from Activity A.

2. Go over the answers as a class.

Activity C Answers, p. 12
1. selection;
2. accuracy;
3. assumptions;
4. predictions;
5. effectively;
6. instinctive;
7. consciously

 For additional practice with suffixes, have students visit *Q Online Practice.*

SPEAKING

Grammar: Auxiliary verbs *do, be, have*
(10 minutes)

1. Read the information about auxiliary verbs. Provide and elicit additional example sentences for students to identify the auxiliary verbs: *Do you often make a good first impression? Is he good at making first impressions? They have not made a good first impression.*

2. Check comprehension by asking questions: *What auxiliary verb do we use in the simple past?* (did) *Which auxiliary verbs do we use in the present perfect?* (has, have) *Which do we use in the simple present?* (do, does) *Which do we use in the present continuous?* (am, is, are) *In the past continuous?* (was, were)

Skill Note

Students should be familiar with the verb forms shown in the book. Point out that it is important to use correct auxiliary forms so that students' English is accurate. To remind them of which auxiliary verbs to use, you may wish to create, or ask students to create, a chart showing the person and number of each subject and the auxiliary verb used for each tense. For example:

Simple present			
I	do	We	do
You	do	You	do
He, she, it	does	They	do

A (10 minutes)

1. Direct students to rewrite the sentences as negative statements.

2. Put students in pairs to discuss their answers.

3. Call on volunteers to share their answers with the class.

Activity A Answers, p. 14
Possible answers:
2. Bill doesn't think first impressions about teachers are usually accurate.
3. Caterina didn't trust her instincts when meeting new people.
4. When Reza buys something, he usually doesn't think/doesn't usually think about it for a long time.

5. Jenny isn't working hard this week.
6. I haven't formed a positive impression of that company.

B (15 minutes)

1. Direct students to work individually to rewrite the sentences as questions.

2. Have them read their questions to a partner. Ask volunteers to write a sentence on the board.

3. Check the questions as a class.

Activity B Answers, p. 15
Possible answers:
2. Do you like talking to new people on the phone?
3. Is Darcy living with people she met last year?
4. Did Marek make lots of friends at school?
5. Did the experts realize the statue was a fake?
6. Has Patrick selected his library books already? / Has Patrick already selected his library books?

 For additional practice with auxiliary verbs *do, be, have,* have students visit *Q Online Practice.*

C (10 minutes)

1. Direct students to work in pairs to ask and answer the questions from Activity B.

2. Point out that for questions students do not know a true answer for, they should use their own ideas.

Pronunciation: Contractions with auxiliary verbs (15 minutes)

CD1, Track 10

1. Read the information about contractions with auxiliary verbs. Write the example sentences used in speech and writing on the board.

2. Check comprehension by asking: *Which words are contracted in each sentence? (She is, They are, Lisa has, We have).*

3. Elicit the verb form in each sentence (present continuous and present perfect).

4. Repeat the process with the sentences for contractions used only in speech.

5. Play the audio as a model for the students. Stop for students to repeat the contracted forms.

6. Point out that in most situations, it is more important for the students to be able to understand contracted speech than to produce it. However, their speech will sound more natural and fluent if they are able to use contracted forms.

A (10 minutes)

🔊 CD1, Track 11

1. Have students listen to the sentences with contractions. Pause after each sentence to give students time to write.

2. Elicit the answers from volunteers. If there are any disagreements, play the audio again to confirm.

> **Activity A Answers, p. 16**
> **1.** is; **2.** did; **3.** is; **4.** has; **5.** have; **6.** did; **7.** have

B (5 minutes)

1. Put students in pairs. Ask them to say the sentences from Activity A using the full form of the auxiliary verbs.

2. Have students practice saying the sentences with contractions. Monitor and provide feedback on pronunciation.

 For additional practice with contractions with auxiliary verbs, have students visit *Q Online Practice*.

▶ *Listening and Speaking 3, page 17*

Speaking Skill:
Taking conversational turns (5 minutes)

🔊 CD1, Track 12

1. Direct students to read the information about taking turns in conversation. Point out that the rules for turn taking in other cultures may be similar to those for American English, or they may be different.

2. Play the audio. Encourage students to repeat the questions.

3. Check comprehension: *What two things does turn taking do?* (It keeps the conversation going and shows that you are interested) *Can you think of any other questions to use?*

4. Give students an opportunity to comment on how turn taking may be similar or different in their cultures.

A (10 minutes)

1. Direct students to look at the conversation. Point out that the conversation is between two classmates, Tony and Alex. Explain that even friends will use polite turn-taking strategies.

2. Put students in pairs to complete the conversation. Point out that more than one question may be possible.

3. Give the pairs time to practice their conversation.

4. Call on volunteers to perform their conversation for the class.

> **Activity A Answers, p. 17**
> Students may choose a variety of the questions from the speaking skills box.

B (10 minutes)

1. Read the questions aloud with the students. Elicit any questions students may have.

2. Give students a few minutes to write their answers to the questions in their notebooks.

3. Put students in pairs to have a conversation about each question.

4. Remind students to take turns and use the questions from the skills box to signal their partner's turn.

5. Monitor students' conversations. Be sure they are taking three turns each.

Expansion Activity:
First Impressions in Conversations (10 minutes)

1. Part of making a good first impression is being able to talk easily with people. Taking conversational turns will help you make a good first impression when you are talking to someone for the first time.

2. As a class, brainstorm additional follow-up questions to keep a conversation going. Write these questions on the board.

3. Conduct a mingling activity. Have the students stand and find a partner. Tell them to pretend they are meeting this person for the first time and want to make a good impression by showing that they are interested in what their partner is saying.

4. Call time after 30 seconds and tell students to find a new partner and start another conversation. Repeat the activity until students have spoken to four or five partners.

 For additional practice with taking turns, have students visit *Q Online Practice*.

Listening and Speaking 3, page 18

Unit Assignment: Give a short talk

Unit Question (5 minutes)

Refer students to the ideas they discussed at the beginning of the unit about whether first impressions are accurate. Cue students if necessary by asking specific questions about the content of the unit: *What are some of the proverbs we discussed about first impressions? What are some of the things that a person does that help us to make our first impression of them? What did you learn about first impressions? Are they ever accurate?*

Learning Outcome

1. Tie the unit assignment to the unit learning outcome. Say: *The outcome for this unit is to describe an inaccurate first impression in detail. This unit assignment is going to let you show your skill in giving a short talk about a time when a first*

impression you made was inaccurate. Being able to analyze your opinions, especially when they are not accurate, is a useful skill in the classroom and on the job.

2. Explain that you are going to use a rubric similar to their Self-Assessment checklist on page 20 of the student book to grade their unit assignment.

▶ *Listening and Speaking 3, page 18*
Consider the Ideas (10 minutes)

1. Direct students to look at the chart. Ask a volunteer to read the characteristics in the first column. Explain that students should write down two additional characteristics that people may notice when forming a first impression.

2. Direct students to rate each of the characteristics by putting a check in the appropriate column. Remind them to rate the two characteristics they thought of.

3. Put students in pairs to compare and discuss their opinions.

   Consider the Ideas Answers, p. 18
   Answers will vary. Students should be able to give reasons for their answers.

▶ *Listening and Speaking 3, page 19*
Prepare and Speak

Gather Ideas

A (10 minutes)

1. Direct students to read the prompt. Ask: *What is brainstorming? Why do we brainstorm?* (It is generating ideas. We do it to generate as many ideas as possible.)

2. Point out that when we brainstorm, we write all of our ideas, including the ones that we are not sure are very good. Have students write as much as they can about the situation and their thoughts in five minutes. Encourage them to write without stopping to correct any grammar errors or erase any content that they are unsure about.

Organize Ideas

B (10 minutes)

1. Have students transfer the information from their brainstorming session into their books.

2. Elicit the features of writing good notes. Ask: *Do we want to write complete sentences? Do we need to write articles such as* an *or* the *in notes? Can we use abbreviations?*

3. Remind students that organization is an important part of preparing a talk. Give them time to review their content in the organizational structure.

4. Ask students if they have used any words with any of the suffixes learned earlier in the unit. Write these words on the board and underline the suffixes.

▶ *Listening and Speaking 3, page 20*

Speak

C (10–15 minutes)

1. Review the Self-Assessment checklist on page 20. Remind students that they will be completing this checklist after their talk.

2. Put students in pairs to give their talks. If time permits, call on volunteers to give their presentations to the class.

3. Use the Unit Assignment Rubric on page 12 of this *Teacher's Handbook* to score each student's talk.

4. Alternatively, divide the class into large groups and have students tell their stories to their group. Have listeners complete the Unit Assignment Rubric.

Alternative Unit Assignments

Assign or have students choose one of these assignments to do instead of, or in addition, to the unit assignment.

1. Tell a partner about a place you have visited. Was your first impression accurate? Explain why or why not.

2. Tell a partner, group, or the class about someone you admire. Describe your first impression of this person, and what you know about him or her now.

 For an additional Unit Assignment, have students visit *Q Online Practice*.

Check and Reflect

Check

A (5 minutes)

1. Direct students to read and complete the Self-Assessment checklist.

2. Ask for a show of hands for how many students gave all or mostly yes answers.

3. Congratulate them on their success. Discuss the steps they can take if an item on the checklist was difficult for them. For example, if they had trouble using contractions, they should practice this skill whenever they get a chance, recording themselves and self-assessing or asking a friend to listen for their pronunciation of contractions.

Reflect

B (5 minutes)

Refer students to the learning outcome on page 3. Tell them to talk with their partners about whether they achieved the learning outcome. Elicit the answers to the unit question that students came up with at the beginning of class. Encourage them to flip through the unit as they discuss the new things they learned and new answers they may have to the unit question.

▶ *Listening and Speaking 3, page 21*

Track Your Success (5 minutes)

1. Have students circle the words they have learned in this unit. Suggest that students go back through the unit to review any words they have forgotten.

2. Have students check the skills they have mastered. If students need more practice in order to feel confident about their proficiency in a skill, point out the page numbers and encourage them to review.

3. Read the learning outcome aloud. Ask students if they felt that they have met the outcome.

Unit Assignment Rubric

Student name: _____

Date: _____

Unit Assignment: *Give a short talk.*

20 = Presentation element was completely successful (at least 90% of the time).
15 = Presentation element was mostly successful (at least 70% of the time).
10 = Presentation element was partially successful (at least 50% of the time).
 0 = Presentation element was not successful.

Give a short talk	20 points	15 points	10 points	0 points
Student spoke easily (without long pauses or reading) and was easy to understand (spoke clearly and at a good speed) when describing an inaccurate first impression in detail.				
Student used correct suffix endings where appropriate.				
Student used contracted forms with auxiliary verbs.				
Student used vocabulary from the unit.				
Student presented content in a coherent and organized manner.				

Total points: _____

Comments:

Unit QUESTION
What's more important: taste or nutrition?

Food and Taste

LISTENING • listening for causes and effects
VOCABULARY • adjective–noun collocations
GRAMMAR • quantifiers with count/noncount nouns
PRONUNCIATION • links with /j/ and /w/
SPEAKING • giving advice

LEARNING OUTCOME

Interview classmates to inform a group discussion on why people prefer certain foods.

▶ *Listening and* **Speaking 3, pages 22–23**
Preview the Unit

Learning Outcome

1. Ask for a volunteer to read the unit skills and then the unit learning outcome.

2. Explain: *The learning outcome is what you are expected to be able to do by the unit's end. You are going to be evaluated for how well you meet this outcome. With this in mind, you should focus on learning skills (Listening, Vocabulary, Grammar, Pronunciation, Speaking) that will support your goal of interviewing classmates to inform a group discussion on why people prefer certain foods. This can also help you act as mentors in the classroom to help the other students meet this outcome.*

A (10 minutes)

1. Prepare students for thinking about the topic by telling them about the foods you prefer. Elicit students' food preferences.

2. Put students in pairs or small groups to discuss the first three questions.

3. Call on volunteers to share their ideas with the class. Ask questions to facilitate the discussion: *Do you have any family traditions that include specific food? Are you aware of the health value of some of your favorite food? Do you drink coffee? Do you think it is healthy? Why or why not?*

4. Focus students' attention on the photo. Have a volunteer describe the photo. Read the last question aloud. Ask: *What are the men doing? Why?*

Activity A Answers, p. 23
Possible answers:
1. Students may mention that food is simply fuel for the body, or they may say that it is a way to enjoy life, comfort themselves, or spend time with friends.

2. Students may think that food that tastes good is high in fat or has a lot of sugar.
3. The men are tasting coffee. They might be labeling coffee according to flavor and strength.

B (15 minutes)

1. Introduce the Unit Question, "What's more important: taste or nutrition?" Ask related information questions or questions about personal experience to help students prepare for answering the Unit Question, which is more abstract. *How important is the taste of food to you? Would you eat less of a favorite food if you knew it wasn't healthy? Do you view food as fuel for your body or is it something that is meant to be enjoyed?*

2. Tell students, *Let's start off our discussion by listing food we think tastes great, for example, ice cream.* Remind students to be specific. It is more helpful to list specific foods than general categories, e.g., *broccoli* or *carrots* instead of *vegetables*.

3. Seat students in small groups and direct them to pass around a paper as quickly as they can, with each group member adding one item to the list. Tell them they have two minutes to make the list and they should write as many items as possible.

4. Call time and ask a reporter from each group to read the list aloud.

5. Use items from the list as a springboard for discussion. For example: *Let's talk about ice cream. Is it nutritious? Why or why not?* Tell students to check the items that the class generally feels are healthy.

Activity B Answers, p. 23
Possible answers: The value of nutrition outweighs the value of good taste. It's important that one's diet consist mainly of nutritious food with occasional tasty treats; Nutrition is more important than taste. We need good nutrition in order to be healthy. Good taste does not help our bodies stay fit and strong.

The Q Classroom
CD1, Track 13

1. Play *The Q Classroom*. Use the example from the audio to help students continue the conversation. Ask: *How did the students answer the question? Do you agree or disagree with their ideas? Why?*

2. On the audio, the students give different opinions about the importance of nutrition versus taste. Elicit the range of student opinion.

3. Remind students of Felix's opinion. He believes people value taste over nutrition, so it is important that food tastes good. Brainstorm a list of nutritious food that tastes good.

▶ *Listening and Speaking 3, page 24*

C (15 minutes)

1. Call on a volunteer to read the introductory paragraph. If necessary, provide the pronunciation of *umami*: \ü-'mä-mē\.

2. Elicit the five tastes. Write them in a row on the board (*sweet, sour, salty, bitter, umami*).

3. Ask students to complete the chart individually and check their favorite foods.

4. Put students in pairs to compare their answers.

5. Have volunteers write the foods in the columns on the board. Discuss the answers as a class. Note that nuts are not naturally salty.

Activity C Answers, p. 24
sweet: ice cream, bananas, pineapple; sour: grapefruit, lemon, pickle; salty: potato chips, nuts; bitter: coffee, parsley, radish; umami: chicken

---

MULTILEVEL OPTION

Group lower-level students and assist them with the task. After higher-level students have checked answers in pairs, tell the pairs to list as many foods for each category as they can. Encourage them to look for patterns, e.g., what categories are fruits in?

D (10 minutes)

1. Put students in groups to discuss the chart on the board and their own individual charts.

2. Have students add one item to each category.

3. Ask a reporter from each group to share the group's chart with the class. Discuss foods that can fall into several categories, for example, pickles can be sour, sweet, or salty.

4. Ask each group to contribute one food item to one of the taste categories. Accept other classifications of the food if they can be supported.

Activity D Answers, p. 24
Student answers may vary. Some foods can fall into several categories like pickles, dark chocolate, or yogurt.

E (10 minutes)

1. Keep students in groups. Ask them to check their favorite food in the chart.

2. Tell students to check their favorite of the five basic tastes.

3. Ask students to compare their preferences with their group members.

4. Ask students to raise their hand for their favorite taste. Say each taste aloud and tally the number of hands for each. Write the numbers on the board.

Expansion Activity:
Taste or Nutrition in Food Categories (10 minutes)

1. Keep students in their groups from Activity E.

2. Tell students to look at the foods listed under each category. With their group, students should decide if the food is known for being nutritious (i.e., broccoli) or for tasting good (i.e., ice cream.)

3. Ask: *Do some categories have more nutritious foods than other categories? Are most of the foods in your favorite category nutritious?*

4. Elicit answers from the groups.

LISTENING

▶ *Listening and Speaking 3, page 25*

LISTENING 1: You Are What You Eat

VOCABULARY (15 minutes)

1. Direct students to read the words and their definitions. Elicit any difficulties or questions.

2. Ask students to complete the sentences.

3. Put students in pairs to check their answers.

4. Ask for volunteers to read the sentences aloud. Provide corrections where necessary.

MULTILEVEL OPTION

Group lower-level students and assist them with the task. Point out the cues in the sentences that will help them to choose the correct word. For example, in the first sentence, the blank follows *my,* so the missing word is either an adjective or a noun. Give them additional sentences to help them practice the difficult vocabulary. For example: *We are not permitted to **consume** food or drink in the library. Don't talk to me now. I am in a very bad **mood**. Athletes eat food with a lot of **calories** because they need a lot of energy.*

Have higher-level students complete the activity individually and then compare answers in pairs. Tell the pairs to write another sample sentence for each word. Have volunteers write one of their sentences on the board. Check the sentences as a class, focusing on the use of vocabulary rather than grammatical issues.

Vocabulary Answers, p. 25
1. diet;	**2.** consume;	**3.** rely on;
4. calories;	**5.** mood;	**6.** spicy;
7. wise;	**8.** mix;	**9.** concentrate;
10. balanced		

 For additional practice with the vocabulary, have students visit *Q Online Practice.*

▶ *Listening and Speaking 3, page 26*
PREVIEW LISTENING 1 (5 minutes)

1. Elicit the meaning of "You Are What You Eat." Explain that it means that our diets are a big part of who we are in that they affect our fitness, energy level, and overall health.

2. Read the introductory paragraph aloud.

3. Have students list foods in their diet that have good effects and foods that have bad effects. Tell students they should review their lists after the listening.

Preview Listening 1 Answers, p. 26
Possible answers: Students may say that sweets and high-calories foods have bad effects because they make them gain weight; they may say that vegetables and fruits have good effects because they give them more energy.

Listening 1 Background Note

The listening stresses the importance of balance in one's diet. There have been many efforts to advise people on how to achieve a balance that is nutritionally sound as well as appealing. One approach encourages people to choose a colorful diet. It is possible to balance one's diet by including a variety of fruits and vegetables from the range of natural colors. For example, yellow/green foods such as spinach and avocado help maintain good vision. Similarly, red/purple foods, like berries and grapes, help our heart function.

LISTEN FOR MAIN IDEAS (5 minutes)

 CD1, Track 14

1. Ask students to look at the chart. Elicit any questions about it. Confirm that students understand the task by asking a volunteer to explain the procedure to you.

2. Play the audio while students complete the chart individually.

3. Elicit the answers. Correct as necessary.

Main Idea Answers, p. 26
1. OK;	**2.** Better;	**3.** OK;	**4.** OK;
5. Better;	**6.** Bad;	**7.** Bad;	**8.** OK

LISTEN FOR DETAILS (10 minutes)

 CD1, Track 15

1. Direct students to read the items before they listen again. Elicit any questions about them.

2. Play the audio while students listen and choose the correct answer.

3. Have students compare answers with a partner.

4. Replay the audio so they can check the answers.

5. Go over the answers with the class.

Listen for Details Answers, p. 26
1. c;	**2.** c;	**3.** a;	**4.** b;	**5.** a;
6. c;	**7.** b;	**8.** b;	**9.** a	

 For additional practice with listening comprehension, have students visit *Q Online Practice.*

▶ *Listening and Speaking 3, page 27*
Q WHAT DO YOU THINK? (10 minutes)

1. Ask students to read the questions and reflect on their answers.

2. Seat students in small groups and assign roles: a group leader to make sure everyone contributes, a note-taker to record the group's ideas, a reporter to share the group's ideas with the class, and a timekeeper to watch the clock.

3. Give students five minutes to discuss the questions. Call time if conversations are winding down. Allow them an extra minute or two if necessary.

4. Call on each group's reporter to share ideas with the class.

> **What Do You Think? Answers, p. 27**
> Students' answers may vary. Possible answers:
> 1. Yes, I think it's important to eat a balanced diet; No, I think her diet suggestions are too strict.
> 2. Yes, people should just eat what they like and worry less about "eating right"; No, nutrition is very important to maintain good health.
> 3. Yes, what you eat affects how you will feel and behave. No, food does not have that much affect on your body.

Learning Outcome

Use the learning outcome to frame the purpose and relevance of Listening 1. Ask: *What did you learn from Listening 1 that prepares you to interview classmates about why people prefer certain foods? What did you learn that will help you to inform a group discussion on food preferences?*

▶ *Listening and Speaking 3, page 28*

Listening Skill: Listening for causes and effects (10 minutes)

🔊 CD1, Track 16

1. Ask students to read the information about causes and effects. Elicit any difficulties or questions.

2. Tell students they are going to hear some examples of cause and effect. Ask them to read along while they listen.

3. Check comprehension by asking questions: *What words and phrases that signal cause and effect? How are* due to *and* because of *different from* since, as, because, *and* so?

A (5 minutes)
🔊 CD1, Track 17

1. Ask students to read the sentences.

2. Play the audio while students complete the sentences.

3. Call on a volunteer to give the answers.

> **Activity A Answers, p. 28**
> **1.** Since; **2.** because of; **3.** Because; **4.** so

▶ *Listening and Speaking 3, page 29*

B (10 minutes)
🔊 CD1, Track 18

1. Tell students they are going to hear four cause and effect statements.

2. Point out that two causes and two effects are printed in the book. Ask a volunteer to read them aloud.

3. Play the audio while students complete the sentences and circle the linking words.

4. Put students in pairs to compare their answers.

5. Call on volunteers to read their answers.

> **Activity B Answers, p. 29**
> **2. so** it's good for your teeth;
> **3. due to** the caffeine;
> **4. since** they have no nutrition at all.

C (5 minutes)

1. Keep students in pairs. Tell them to read the directions. Elicit any difficulties with questions.

2. Call on a volunteer to read the examples in blue. Elicit the cause and effect of each statement, as well as the linking word.

3. Ask students to write their sentences individually and then share them with their partner.

4. Call on several pairs to share their answers.

 For additional practice with listening for causes and effects, have students visit *Q Online Practice*.

▶ *Listening and Speaking 3, page 30*

LISTENING 2: Food Tasters

VOCABULARY (10 minutes)

1. Ask students to locate the bold words in each sentence. Pronounce and have students repeat the words.

2. Have students read the sentences and choose the correct answer for each. Call on volunteers to read the answers aloud.

> **Vocabulary Answers, p. 30**
> **1.** a; **2.** c; **3.** c; **4.** c; **5.** b;
> **6.** c; **7.** c; **8.** b; **9.** a; **10.** a

Group lower-level students and assist them with the task. Point out the cues in the sentences that will help them to choose the correct word.

Have higher-level students complete the activity individually and then compare answers in pairs. Tell the pairs to write another sample sentence for each word. Have volunteers write one of their sentences on the board. Check the sentences as a class, focusing on the use of vocabulary rather than grammatical issues.

 For additional practice with the vocabulary, have students visit *Q Online Practice*.

▶ *Listening and Speaking 3, page 31*

PREVIEW LISTENING 2 (5 minutes)

Direct students' attention to the photos and ask: *Why might a food taster taste cheese? What other foods do you think a food taster might try? Why?*

Listening 2 Background Note

Many food production companies employ food tasters. These people typically have educational backgrounds in food science or production development and marketing. Food tasters can specialize in one food, for example, chocolate, cheese, beef, or coffee.

LISTEN FOR MAIN IDEAS (10 minutes)

 CD1, Track 19

Ask students to read the statements about each person. Elicit any difficulties with vocabulary or concepts. Play the audio and have students write *T* or *F* individually.

> **Listen for Main Idea Answers, p. 32**
> **1.** T; **2.** F; **3.** F; **4.** F; **5.** T;
> **6.** T; **7.** T; **8.** T; **9.** T

▶ *Listening and Speaking 3, page 32*

LISTEN FOR DETAILS (5 minutes)

 CD1, Track 20

1. Ask students to look at the chart before they listen again.

2. As you play the audio, have students write the letter of the name next to the correct information.

3. Have students compare answers with a partner.

4. Check answers with the class.

> **Listen for Details Answers, p. 32**
> **Jobs:** cheese buyer M; coffee taster E; chocolate taster S
> **Type of business:** important company E; supermarket M; department store S
> **Locations:** Los Angeles E; London S; near Paris M

 For additional practice with listening comprehension, have students visit *Q Online Practice*.

WHAT DO YOU THINK?

A (10 minutes)

1. Ask students to read the questions and reflect on their answers.

2. Seat students in small groups and assign roles: a group leader to make sure everyone contributes, a note-taker to record the group's ideas, a reporter to share the group's ideas with the class, and a timekeeper to watch the clock.

3. Give students five minutes to discuss the questions. Call time if conversations are winding down. Allow them an extra minute or two if necessary.

4. Call on each group's reporter to share ideas with the class.

> **Activity A Answers, p. 32**
> Students' answers may vary. Possible answers:
> **1.** Cheese, because I love salty flavors.
> **2.** Yes, I would love to eat all day; No, I would gain too much weight.

B (5 minutes)

1. Have students continue working their small groups to discuss the questions in Activity B. Tell them to choose a new leader, recorder, reporter, and timekeeper.

2. Encourage students to make a list of issues for each food and food taster.

3. Call on the new reporter to share the group's answers to the questions.

> **Activity B Answers, p. 31**
> Students' answers will vary. Possible answers:
> **1.** Enrique, because of the caffeine.
> **2.** Marie, because cheese has a lot of salt.

Tip for Critical Thinking (1 minute)

Read the tip aloud. Point out that making predictions is something we do every day, but we are not often aware of the thought process that goes into making a prediction. By being aware of what clues and factors influence our predictions, we can improve their accuracy.

Critical Q: Expansion Activity

Making informed predictions

1. Tell students they are going to make predictions about what would happen to them if they changed their diets. Ask them to list what they have eaten over the past two days.

2. Ask students to think about what they learned in the listenings about a good diet. Have them analyze their food choices.

3. Tell students to predict what would happen if they changed their diet to follow the advice in the listenings. Tell them to consider not only the repercussions on their health, but also on their lifestyle and finances.

4. Put students in pairs to share their predictions. Encourage them to ask their partner for details and explanations.

5. Call on volunteers to share their predictions and reasons with the class.

Learning Outcome

Use the learning outcome to frame the purpose and relevance of Listenings 1 and 2 and the Critical Q activity of making predictions. Ask: *What did you learn from Listening 1 that prepares you to interview classmates about why people prefer certain foods? What did you learn that will help you to inform a group discussion on food preferences?*

▶ *Listening and Speaking 3, page 33*

Vocabulary Skill: Adjective–noun collocations (5 minutes)

1. Direct students to read the information silently.

2. Read the sentences aloud to model correct stress and pronunciation. Have students repeat.

3. Check comprehension: *What is a collocation? Which word comes first, the adjective or the noun? Why should students use collocations?*

Skill Note

Remind students that adjective-noun collocations are very common in English. Point out that some adjectives tend to collocate with some nouns and it is important to remember them. For example, although

fast and *quick* are synonyms, we do not say *quick food*. Encourage students to keep a list of adjectives or nouns and their common collocations.

A (5 minutes)

Put students in pairs or small groups to complete the collocations. Go over the answers with the class.

> **Activity A Answers, p. 33**
> **1.** a soft drink; **2.** junk food; **3.** a juicy steak;
> **4.** a balanced diet; **5.** a quick snack

B (10 minutes)

1. Have students complete the sentences individually.

2. Have students check their answers with their partners or group. Check answers as a class.

> **Activity B Answers, p. 34**
> **1.** juicy steak; **2.** a balanced diet; **3.** a soft drink;
> **4.** junk food; **5.** a quick snack

▶ *Listening and Speaking 3, page 34*

C (5 minutes)

1. Have pairs or groups complete the sentences.

2. Go over the answers as a class. Point out that although some of the answer choices have similar meanings, for example, *filthy* and *dirty*, the correct answers are the most common collocations.

> **Activity C Answers, p. 34**
> **1.** a; **2.** b; **3.** b; **4.** b; **5.** a

 For additional practice with adjective-noun collocations, have students visit *Q Online Practice*.

▶ *Listening and Speaking 3, page 35*

SPEAKING

Grammar: Quantifiers with count/noncount nouns (10 minutes)

1. Read the information about count and noncount nouns. Write the words *count* and *noncount* on the board. Elicit additional examples of each noun. For example, *count: banana, chair, pen; noncount: sugar, money, plastic.*

2. Check comprehension by asking questions: *Do we use* too much *or* too many *with the noun* money? *Are* too much *and* too many *used when we have the right amount of something?*

Skill Note

Count and noncount nouns are frequently taught with food items because there is a range of both count and noncount nouns in this category. You may wish to use items in the food category to present this point. Give sentences for students to complete. For example:

*I ruined the soup! I put **too much** salt in.*

*My tea is perfect. There is **enough** sugar in it.*

***How many** bananas are in this recipe?*

A (10 minutes)

1. Ask students to look at the photo. Ask: *What are those? Are they spicy or sweet?*

2. Direct students to complete the conversations with the words and phrases from the box.

3. Put students in pairs to check their answers. Check the answers as a class.

4. Have students practice the conversations.

> **Activity A Answers, p. 35**
> **1.** many; **2.** enough; **3.** too many;
> **4.** much; **5.** not enough; **6.** too much

Listening and Speaking 3, page 36

B (10 minutes)

1. Read the directions aloud. Have students complete the activity.

2. Put students in pairs. Tell them to discuss their partner's food preferences.

3. Encourage students to ask follow-up questions, for example: *How much sugar do you like in your coffee? How many times a week do you eat your favorite food?*

4. Call on volunteers to report their partner's information.

> **Activity B Answers, p. 36**
> Answers will vary. Students should correctly list C or N next to their food choices.

 For additional practice with count and noncount nouns, have students visit *Q Online Practice*.

Tip for Success (1 minute)

Read the tip aloud. Remind students that in addition to maintaining eye contact, some people will nod their heads or smile to show that they are engaged in the conversation.

Listening and Speaking 3, page 37

Pronunciation: Links with /j/ and /w/ (10 minutes)

CD1, Track 21

1. Read the information about linking sounds. Write the linking sounds /j/ and /w/ and the vowel sounds they link on the board. Say the sounds and have students repeat after you.

2. Check comprehension by asking: *What sound connects these words,* Monday is? *What sound connects these words,* go over?

3. Have students read along while they listen to the audio. Stop for students to repeat the linking sounds.

4. Point out that linking is a feature of fluent speech in formal and informal situations. Encourage students to think of the two words as one in order to make the linking sounds.

A (10 minutes)
CD1, Track 22

1. Have students read the sentences. Point out that there may be more than one linking sound in each.

2. Have students mark the linking sounds they expect to hear in the sentences. Play the audio while students check their predictions.

3. Elicit the answers from volunteers. Play the audio again.

> **Activity A Answers, p. 37**
> **1.** We /j/ all eat things we know we shouldn't.
> **2.** "Empty" calories have no nutritional value /w/ at all.
> **3.** I can't drink coffee, but tea /j/ is fine.
> **4.** Cheese has calcium, so /w/ it's good for your teeth.
> **5.** Sometimes in the /j/ evening I'm too /w/ tired to cook.
> **6.** Marie makes sure the cheese is ready to go /w/ out on sale.
> **7.** Stuart thinks the /j/ appearance of chocolate can be /j/ as important as the taste.
> **8.** Enrique thinks people pay /j/ a lot for coffee, so they want to /w/ enjoy /j/ it.

B (10 minutes)
CD1, Track 23

1. Put students in pairs to say the sentences from Activity A.

2. Have students practice saying the sentences with linking. Monitor and provide feedback.

3. Play the audio again, pausing for students to repeat the linking sounds.

 For additional practice with linking /j/ and /w/, have students visit *Q Online Practice*.

▶ *Listening and Speaking 3, page 38*

Speaking Skill: Giving advice (10 minutes)

🔊 CD1, Track 24

1. Direct students to read the information about giving advice.

2. Play the audio. Encourage students to repeat the sentences.

3. Check comprehension: *What words do we use to give advice? What word do we use to make advice stronger? How can we make advice more polite?*

21ST CENTURY SKILLS

Interviewing people is something students will do in their professional and academic lives. Most students forget that an interview is a conversation and they tend to focus solely on asking questions and writing answers. Good interviewers listen and show flexibility. Help students develop interview flexibility through practice. Tell students to write at least one new question while they are listening to a partner or group member speak. Tell them to ask this follow-up question before moving on to the next new question. This activity will not only help them prepare for unit assignments, but it will also help them develop better interview skills for the future.

A (10 minutes)

1. Ask students to read the directions and sample conversation. Ask them to think about their diet and the things that they think are not good about it. If necessary, ask students to look back at page 36 to the lists of the foods they like and don't like.

2. Put students in pairs to discuss their diets and give advice.

3. Call on volunteers to share some of their eating habits and advice for each other.

B (10 minutes)

1. Put students in groups to share the advice they received. Have a volunteer read the examples aloud.

2. Remind students to maintain eye contact and use the strategies for taking turns presented in Unit 1.

3. Monitor students' conversations for their use of count/noncount nouns and ways of giving advice.

 For additional practice with giving advice, have students visit *Q Online Practice*.

▶ *Listening and Speaking 3, page 39*

Unit Assignment: Conduct a class survey

Unit Question (5 minutes)

Refer students to the ideas they discussed at the beginning of the unit about why people prefer certain foods. Cue students if necessary by asking specific questions about the content of the unit: *Why do some people prefer nutritious foods to delicious foods? What kinds of foods should we eat? What is a balanced diet? Can a balanced diet include chocolate?*

Learning Outcome

1. Tie the unit assignment to the unit learning outcome. Say: *The outcome for this unit is to interview classmates to inform a group discussion on why people prefer certain foods. This unit assignment is going to let you show your skill in conducting a survey which will inform a group discussion on the topic of food preferences. Conducting a survey is a useful way to collect information or conduct research.*

2. Explain that you are going to use a rubric similar to their Self-Assessment checklist on page 42 to grade their unit assignment.

Consider the Ideas (10 minutes)

1. Put students in groups to match the food to the country it comes from. Explain that students should use their best guesses.

2. Review the answers with the class.

3. Ask students to discuss which dishes they like and which they don't like.

4. Direct students to discuss other dishes from around the world that they have tried. Tell them to quiz each other on where different dishes come from.

5. Call on volunteers to share their information with the whole class.

Consider the Ideas Answers, p. 39
1. c; **2.** f; **3.** b; **4.** d; **5.** a; **6.** e.

▶ *Listening and Speaking 3, page 40*
Prepare and Speak

Gather Ideas

A (5 minutes)

Direct students to read the prompt and list their favorite dishes. Encourage them to choose dishes that they have had or prepared many times.

Organize Ideas

B (10 minutes)

1. Have students choose a dish from Activity A.

2. Remind students that organization is an important part of preparing a talk.

3. Encourage students to make their best guess if they are unsure about the ingredients or the healthful benefits of the dish.

▶ *Listening and Speaking 3, page 41*
Tip for Success (1 minute)

Read the tip aloud. Elicit the features of writing good notes. Ask: *Do we want to write complete sentences? Do we need to write articles such as, an or the in notes? Should we use abbreviations?*

Speak

C (10–15 minutes)

1. Put students in groups to interview each other.

2. Remind students not to read their information from Activity B. Encourage them to maintain eye contact and only refer to their notes as necessary.

3. Monitor students' interviewing and answering techniques.

4. Use the Unit Assignment Rubric on page 22 of this *Teacher's Handbook* to score each student's interview and answer.

5. Alternatively, have other group members listen to each other's interviews and answers. Have listeners complete the Unit Assignment Rubric.

6. Have groups summarize the information from their interviews.

7. Ask a reporter from each group to present the group's findings.

Alternative Unit Assignments

Assign or have students choose one of these assignments to do instead of or in addition to the unit assignment.

1. In a small group, talk about the role of food in popular holidays and festivals in your country. What food do people eat at celebrations? Is it healthy or unhealthy?

2. Think about a recipe for a dish you know and love. Make notes of the ingredients, and how to cook it. Then tell each other your recipes.

 For an additional unit assignment, have students visit *Q Online Practice*.

▶ *Listening and Speaking 3, page 42*
Check and Reflect

Check

A (5 minutes)

1. Direct students to read and complete the Self-Assessment checklist.

2. Ask for a show of hands for how many students gave all or mostly yes answers.

3. Congratulate them on their success. Discuss the steps they can take if an item on the rubric was difficult for them.

Reflect

B (5 minutes)

Refer students to the learning outcome on page 23. Tell them to talk with their partners about whether they achieved the learning outcome. Elicit the answers to the Unit Question that students came up with at the beginning of class. Encourage them to flip through the unit as they discuss the new things they learned and new answers they may have to the Unit Question.

▶ *Listening and Speaking 3, page 43*
Track Your Success

1. Have students circle the words they have learned in this unit.

2. Have students check the skills they have mastered. If students need more practice in order to feel confident about their proficiency in a skill, point out the page numbers and encourage them to review.

3. Read the learning outcome aloud. Ask students if they feel that they have met the outcome.

Unit Assignment Rubric

Student name: _____

Date: _____

Unit Assignment: *Conduct a class survey.*

20 = Presentation element was completely successful (at least 90% of the time).
15 = Presentation element was mostly successful (at least 70% of the time).
10 = Presentation element was partially successful (at least 50% of the time).
 0 = Presentation element was not successful.

Conduct a class survey	20 points	15 point	10 point	0 point
Student spoke easily (without long pauses or reading) while discussing why people prefer certain foods and was easy to understand (spoke clearly and at a good speed).				
Student used /j/ and /w/ for linking.				
Student used count and noncount nouns correctly.				
Student used vocabulary from the unit.				
Student elicited relevant information from other students during the interview phase.				

Total points: _____

Comments:

Unit QUESTION

What can we learn from success and failure?

Success

LISTENING • listening for examples
VOCABULARY • prefixes
GRAMMAR • gerunds and infinitives as the objects of verbs
PRONUNCIATION • stress on important words
SPEAKING • asking for and giving clarification

LEARNING OUTCOME

Discuss successful and unsuccessful personal experiences and explain what you learned from them.

▶ *Listening and Speaking 3, pages 44–45*

Preview the Unit

Learning Outcome

1. Ask for a volunteer to read the unit skills and then the unit learning outcome.

2. Explain: *The learning outcome is what you are expected to be able to do by the unit's end. You are going to be evaluated for how well you meet this outcome. With this in mind, you should focus on learning skills (Listening, Vocabulary, Grammar, Pronunciation, Speaking) that will support your goal of discussing successful and unsuccessful personal experiences and explaining what you learned from these experiences. This can also help you act as mentors in the classroom to help the other students meet this outcome.*

A (10 minutes)

1. Prepare students for thinking about the topic by eliciting a class definition of success. Accept all students' contributions and refine the definition accordingly.

2. Put students in pairs or small groups to discuss the first two questions.

3. Call on volunteers to share their ideas with the class. Ask questions: *Did your discussion confirm your definition of success or not? What are some of the ways in which you are successful? How do you personally define success?*

4. Focus students' attention on the photo. Have a volunteer describe the photo to the class. Read the question aloud. Ask: *What is this man trying to do? Will he be successful? Why or why not?*

Activity A Answers, p. 45

1. Students may say a person can be successful by earning a lot of money, by discovering or inventing something, or by being happy and content with their lives.

2. Students should support their answers with specific examples from their lives.

3. The man is trying to fly or glide. He may be successful because the machine looks well-built, or he may not be successful because he lacks the speed to lift off.

B (20 minutes)

1. Introduce the Unit Question, "What can we learn from success and failure?" Ask related information questions or questions about personal experience to help students prepare for answering the Unit Question, which is more abstract. *How important is it to be successful? Is it possible to be successful even in failure? What is failure? How important is it to fail once in a while? Do you think a person's definition of success can change over time? Do you know anyone for whom this has happened?*

2. Put students in small groups and give each group a piece of poster paper and a marker.

3. Give students a minute to silently consider their answers to the Unit Question. Tell students to pass the paper and the marker around the group. Direct each group member to write a different answer to the question. Encourage them to help one another.

4. Ask each group to choose a reporter to read the answers to the class. Point out similarities and differences among the answers. If answers from different groups are similar, make a group list that incorporates all of the answers. Post the list to refer to later in the unit.

Activity B Answers, p. 45
Possible answers: Success and failure can inform us about what we have mastered and what we still need to master; When we succeed, we have achieved a goal and when we fail, we discover the areas in which we need to work harder; Success shows us what we can do and failure shows us what we cannot do yet.

The Q Classroom
🔊 CD1, Track 25

1. Play *The Q Classroom.* Use the example from the audio to help students continue the conversation. Ask: *How did the students answer the question? Do you agree or disagree with their ideas? Why?*

2. On the audio, Sophy gives three areas in which people can be successful. Elicit them and whether all three of them were discussed in Activity A.

3. Also on the audio, the students give different opinions about the value of success and the value of failure. Elicit these opinions and the range of student opinions in the class.

▶ *Listening and Speaking 3, page 46*

C (10 minutes)

1. Call on a volunteer to read the meanings of success in the left column. Have students write two additional ideas about what success may mean to someone.

2. Tell students to check the top three items that are most true for them. Have them write a reason for each choice in the space to the right of the list.

Activity C Answers, p. 46
Students' answers will vary. Student should support their choices with valid reasons.

MULTILEVEL OPTION

Group lower-level students and assist them with the task. If necessary, allow them to choose only one or two options from the list. Ask higher-level students to rank all the items from 1 through 11 (with 1 being most true for them). Ask them to write a justification as to why the item is important, moderately important, or not important to them when defining success.

D (10 minutes)

1. Put students in groups to discuss the items they checked in Activity C.

2. Conclude the activity by asking for a show of hands when students hear you read the meaning they ranked first. Read the list aloud. Tally the number for each meaning.

Expansion Activity: How to achieve success
(10 minutes)

1. Keep students in their groups from Activity D.

2. Ask students to consider how they plan to be successful at the things they chose on the questionnaire.

3. Tell them to brainstorm a few ideas for each choice, and to make notes.

4. Have the students discuss their plans to achieve success with their group members. Group members should provide helpful suggestions for their plan.

5. Elicit answers from the group.

LISTENING

▶ *Listening and Speaking 3, page 47*
LISTENING 1: Chasing Your Dreams

VOCABULARY (15 minutes)

1. Model the pronunciation of the words in bold.

2. Put students in pairs to circle the answers. Call on volunteers to read the answers aloud. Elicit or provide corrections as necessary.

MULTILEVEL OPTION

Group lower-level students and assist them with the task. Tell them to substitute the choices they aren't sure of in the sentences to see if the meaning changes. Give them additional sentences to help them practice the difficult vocabulary. For example:
1. This refrigerator is very good, but the **downside** is that it consumes a lot of electricity.
2. You will not be able to **achieve** much in school if you do not study a lot.
3. I find this problem very **frustrating**. I can't figure out the answer.
4. I don't know why you **gave up** so easily. You almost had the answer.
Have higher-level students complete the activity individually and then compare answers in pairs. Tell the pairs to write another sample sentence for each word. Have volunteers write one of their sentences on the board. Check the sentences as a class, focusing on the use of vocabulary rather than grammatical issues.

Vocabulary Answers, p. 47
1. a; **2.** b; **3.** c; **4.** c; **5.** a;
6. b; **7.** a; **8.** b; **9.** c; **10.** a

 For additional practice with the vocabulary, have students visit *Q Online Practice*.

 Listening and Speaking 3, page 48
PREVIEW LISTENING 1 (5 minutes)

1. Elicit the meaning of the title "Chasing your Dreams" (pursuing something you really want).

2. Direct students to look at the photo. Ask: *What definition of success does this car represent? Do you think it's a good symbol for success? Is having a car like this a realistic goal? Why or why not?*

3. Read the introductory paragraph aloud. Have students check the things they think the professor will say are important for achieving success. Students may check as many items as they wish. Tell students to review their lists after the listening.

   Preview the Listening Answers, p. 48
   Students' answers will vary. The item mentioned in the listening is *having clear goals*.

Listening 1 Background Note

This listening focuses on what it really means to be successful. In order to achieve success on their own terms, people around the world have changed careers, set different priorities, or reassessed their values. Ordinary people are doing this, as evidenced by the increasing numbers of fathers who opt to spend time as primary caregivers for their children, as well as the number of people who dedicate themselves to greener living through recycling and gardening.

LISTEN FOR MAIN IDEAS (10 minutes)

 CD1, Track 26

1. Ask students to read the sentences and answer choices. Elicit any questions or difficulties about them.

2. Play the audio and have students choose their answers individually.

3. Elicit the answers from the class.

   Main Idea Answers, p. 48
   1. a; **2.** b; **3.** b; **4.** b

 Listening and Speaking 3, page 49
LISTEN FOR DETAILS (10 minutes)

 CD1, Track 27

1. Direct students to read the statements before they listen again. Elicit any questions about them.

2. As you play the audio, have students listen and write *T* or *F*.

3. Have students compare answers with a partner.

4. Replay the audio so that the partners can check their answers.

5. Go over the answers with the class.

   Listen for Details Answers, p. 49
   1. F; **2.** F; **3.** T; **4.** T; **5.** T; **6.** F; **7.** T

 For additional practice with listening comprehension, have students visit *Q Online Practice*.

WHAT DO YOU THINK? (10 minutes)

1. Ask students to look at the photo and read the caption. Elicit their opinions about the relationship between the photo and the caption. (Success is not just achieving first place, but a personal best, whether that is second, third, or just competing.)

2. Seat students in small groups and assign roles: a group leader to make sure everyone contributes, a note-taker to record the group's ideas, a reporter to share the group's ideas with the class, and a timekeeper to watch the clock.

3. Give students five minutes to discuss the questions. Call time if conversations are winding down. Allow them an extra minute or two if necessary.

4. Call on each group's reporter to share ideas with the class. Remind them to report opinions about the things that are more important than success.

   What Do You Think? Answers, p. 49
   Students' answers may vary. Possible answers:
   1. Yes, it makes sense to be realistic about what you can achieve; No, it's important to dream big.
   2. Students may talk about a friend or family member who has achieved something important in the life.
   3. Good friends, a happy family, being healthy.

Learning Outcome

Use the learning outcome to frame the purpose and relevance of Listening 1. Ask: *What did you learn from Listening 1 that prepares you to discuss successful and unsuccessful personal experiences? What did you learn that will help you to explain what you learned from these experiences?*

▶ *Listening and Speaking 3, page 50*

Listening Skill:
Listening for examples (10 minutes)

1. Ask students to read the information about listening for examples. Elicit any difficulties or questions.

2. Check comprehension by asking: *Why do we need to listen for examples?*

A (5 minutes)
🔊 CD1, Track 28

1. Tell students they are going to listen to the professor's lecture again. Explain that they are just going to focus on listening for the phrases that the professor uses to introduce examples.

2. Play the audio while students write the phrases used to introduce examples. If necessary, pause or replay the audio to give students a chance to write.

3. Call on a volunteer to give the answers.

> **Activity A Answers, p. 50**
> **1.** To give you an example;
> **2.** for instance;
> **3.** Take for example;
> **4.** for example

B (10 minutes)
🔊 CD1, Track 29

1. Tell students they are going to listen to Paul talk about how his view of success has changed.

2. Explain that students should write the examples he gives in note form. Elicit that note form does not require complete sentences or full words.

3. Ask students to read the items. Elicit any questions or difficulties.

4. Play the audio while students write the examples.

5. Put students in pairs to compare their answers.

6. Call on volunteers to read their answers.

> **Activity B Answers, p. 50**
> **1.** only chose jobs that paid well;
> **2.** left one company to work for another (for a better job title);
> **3.** loves jogging (in the park);
> **4.** sees reconnecting with his old college friends as a success.

▶ *Listening and Speaking 3, page 51*

C (10 minutes)

1. Tell students to read the directions. Elicit any difficulties or questions.

2. Model the activity by choosing a goal of your own, writing it on the board, and listing one benefit of achieving it.

3. Give students a minute to think about their goal and its benefits. Students should write their sentences individually.

D (15 minutes)

1. Remind students of the phrases from the listening skills box by eliciting them from the class and writing them on the board.

2. Put students in pairs to share their goals and the benefits they hope to gain. Tell them to take notes while the listen. Review the features of good note-taking.

3. Call on several students to share their partners' goals and benefits. Ask their partner to identify the phrases used to give examples.

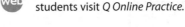 For additional practice with giving examples, have students visit *Q Online Practice*.

▶ *Listening and Speaking 3, page 52*

LISTENING 2: The Benefits of Failure

Tip for Success (1 minute)

1. Read the tip aloud.

2. Point out that knowing a number of synonyms for common words can make students' speech much more interesting, and it can make understanding a variety of speakers in different situations easier.

VOCABULARY (10 minutes)

1. Model the pronunciation of the words. Have students repeat after you.

2. Review the meaning of the letters in parentheses: (n.) = noun, (phr. v.) = phrasal verb, etc.

3. Put students in pairs to circle the answers. Call on volunteers to read the answers aloud.

> **Vocabulary Answers, p. 52**
> **2.** improve; **3.** stress; **4.** be afraid; **5.** need;
> **6.** allow; **7.** training; **8.** leading; **9.** refuse;
> **10.** identify

For additional practice with the vocabulary, have students visit *Q Online Practice*.

PREVIEW LISTENING 2 (5 minutes)

1. Direct students' attention to the photo and ask: *Do you recognize this basketball player? What do you know about Michael Jordan? What else is he known for (Nike shoes and charity work)?*

2. Tell students they are going to listen to a speech by a college student.

3. Give students a minute to write down their ideas about how failure can be a positive experience.

Listening 2 Background Note

When Michael Jordan was cut from his high school basketball team, he improved his game and went on to a successful college, professional, and Olympic career.

John Grisham's first novel, *A Time to Kill*, took three years to write, and was rejected numerous times before being published by a small unknown publishing house. Grisham has written more than five best-selling novels, several of which have been made into films.

Akio Morita was expected to take over the family food business, but his talents were in science and technology. He and his friend Masaru Ibuka founded Sony, which has become one of the world's most successful corporations.

 Listening and Speaking 3, page 53

LISTEN FOR MAIN IDEAS (5 minutes)

 CD1, Track 30

1. Ask students to read the statements. Elicit any difficulties with vocabulary or concepts.

2. Play the audio and have students complete the activity individually. Confirm answers.

Listen for Main Idea Answers, p. 53
Students should check items 2, 4, and 5.

LISTEN FOR DETAILS (10 minutes)

 CD1, Track 31

1. Explain that students are going to listen for specific information about each successful person or group.

2. As you play the audio, have students write the letter of the quote next to the correct name. Tell students to work individually.

3. Have students compare answers with a partner.

4. Go over the answers with the class. Elicit what each person or group was known for.

Listen for Details Answers, p. 53
1. f; **2.** e; **3.** a; **4.** d; **5.** c; **6.** b

 For additional practice with listening comprehension, have students visit *Q Online Practice*.

WHAT DO YOU THINK?

A (10 minutes)

1. Ask students to read the questions and reflect on their answers.

2. Seat students in small groups and assign roles: a group leader to make sure everyone contributes, a note-taker to record the group's ideas, a reporter to share the group's ideas with the class, and a timekeeper to watch the clock.

3. Give students five minutes to discuss the questions. Call time if conversations are winding down. Allow them an extra minute or two if necessary.

4. Call on each group's reporter to share ideas with the class.

Activity A Answers, p. 53
Students' answers will vary. Possible Answers:
1. Students should support their answers with reasons.
2. Student may talk about a class that they did poorly in but then took again and passed or a sports team that they were cut from at first but then tried again and succeeded.

B (5 minutes)

1. Have students continue working their small groups to discuss the questions in Activity B. Tell them to choose a new leader, recorder, reporter, and timekeeper.

2. For question 1, encourage students to make a list of the examples in the speech and discuss each one. For question 2, suggest students record their answer for future reference.

3. Call on the new reporter to share the group's answers to the questions.

> **Activity B Answers, p. 53**
> Students' answers will vary. Possible answers:
> 1. No, Carl Simmons thinks it's OK to pursue goals even when other people think they're unrealistic.
> 2. Success now means more to me than just earning a lot of money.

Learning Outcome

Use the learning outcome to frame the purpose and relevance of Listenings 1 and 2. Ask: *What did you learn from the listenings that prepares you to discuss successful personal experiences? What did you learn that will help you to discuss unsuccessful experiences?*

▶ *Listening and Speaking 3, page 54*

Vocabulary Skill: Prefixes (5 minutes)

1. Direct students to read the information silently.

2. Check comprehension: *What do the prefixes* dis-, im-, *and* ir- *do? When do we use* im- *and when do we use* ir-? *Which prefix means "many"? What prefix means "against"? Can you think of a word that uses this prefix?*

Skill Note

Remind students that just as we have synonyms for many words, there are prefixes with synonymous meanings. The examples in the book are the prefixes *dis-*, *im-*, and *ir-*, which all give the opposite meaning to a word. Point out that knowing the meaning of a prefix can help students figure out the meaning of a word that they are uncertain of. Remind them to use these skills when they are studying.

A (10–15 minutes)

1. Put students in pairs or small groups to complete the activity. Encourage students to use a dictionary if they are unsure.

2. Go over the answers with the class.

> **Activity A Answers, p. 54**
> **1.** review; **2.** irresponsible; **3.** dislike;
> **4.** co-worker; **5.** imperfect; **6.** antisocial;
> **7.** multinational; **8.** dishonest; **9.** impatient;
> **10.** irregular; **11.** reapply; **12.** multimedia

B (5 minutes)

1. Keep students in pairs or groups, but have students write sentences individually.

2. Have students check their answers with the partners or group members. Go over the answers as a class.

> **Activity B Answers, p. 54**
> Students' answers will vary. Students' sentences should correctly use words from Activity A.

MULTILEVEL OPTION

Group lower-level students and assist them with the task. You may wish to give students a sentence and ask them to choose a word from Activity A to complete it. For example,

1. He wasn't accepted at his first choice university this year, but he is going to **reapply** next year.

2. Mother won't give Anna the keys to the car because she thinks she is **irresponsible** and shouldn't drive.

3. If someone is **dishonest**, people don't trust them.

4. My sister doesn't like to go to parties or do things with large groups of people. She is a little bit **antisocial**.

Have higher-level students write sentences for more than three words and then compare answers with a partner. Have volunteers write one of their sentences on the board. Correct the sentences with the whole class, focusing on the use of the vocabulary word rather than other grammatical issues.

C (5 minutes)

1. Keep students in pairs or groups.

2. Ask students to read their sentences to each other again so that they can write the words with prefixes in their notebooks.

 For additional practice with prefixes, have students visit *Q Online Practice*.

▶ *Listening and Speaking 3, page 55*

SPEAKING

Grammar: Gerunds and infinitives as the objects of verbs (10 minutes)

1. Read the information about gerunds and infinitives.

2. Check comprehension by asking questions: *What is the gerund for the verb* run? *What is the infinitive of the verb* walk?

3. Review spelling rules for forming gerunds:

   • Verbs ending in vowel + consonant: double the consonant, e.g., *running, swimming, planning*, etc.

   • Verbs ending in vowel + consonant + *-e*: drop the *e* and add *-ing*, e.g., *hiking, becoming, having*, etc.

Skill Note

Some students may be familiar with a group of verbs that change meaning depending on whether they are followed by a gerund or an infinitive. There are only a few verbs that this applies to. They include: *stop, remember,* and *forget.*

I forgot to write *the note.* (I didn't write the note.)

I forgot writing *the note.* (I wrote the note, but I don't remember doing it.)

A (10 minutes)

1. Tell students to circle the correct verb forms individually.

2. Remind them to look at the grammar note for help.

3. Put students in pairs to check their answers. Check the answers as a class.

4. Have students practice the conversation.

> **Activity A Answers, p. 55**
> **1.** to give; **2.** to become; **3.** being; **4.** working;
> **5.** to quit; **6.** to stay; **7.** to spend; **8.** to have

▶ *Listening and Speaking 3, page 56*

B (15 minutes)

1. Direct students to work individually to answer the questions.

2. Put students in pairs to discuss their answers. Encourage them to ask follow-up questions, for example: *Why do you plan to do this soon? Why didn't you finish? Why don't you have enough time to do this activity now?*

3. Call on volunteers to report their partner's information.

> **Activity B Answers, p. 56**
> Answers will vary. Students should correctly use gerunds and infinitives.

 For additional practice with gerunds and infinitives, have students visit *Q Online Practice.*

Pronunciation: Stress on important words (10 minutes)

 CD1, Track 32

1. Read the information about stressing important words.

2. Check comprehension by asking: *Why are some words stressed? What can listening for stressed words help us to do?*

3. Play the audio as a model for the students. Stop for students to repeat.

A (10 minutes)

CD1, Track 33

1. Have students read the sentences. Point out that, as in the sentences above, there may be more than one word stressed.

2. Ask students to underline the words they expect to hear stressed in the sentences.

3. Play the audio while students check their predictions. Pause after each sentence to give students time to check.

4. Elicit the answers from volunteers. If there are any disagreements, play the audio again to confirm.

> **Activity A Answers, p. 56**
> **1.** <u>Failure</u> is an important <u>stage</u> on the <u>road</u> to <u>success</u>.
> **2.** We <u>shouldn't</u> be <u>afraid</u> of <u>failure</u>, because we can <u>learn</u> from it.
> **3.** <u>Failure</u> is <u>something</u> to be <u>encouraged</u> by.
> **4.** <u>Don't</u> give <u>up</u> too <u>easily</u>!

▶ *Listening and Speaking 3, page 57*

B (5 minutes)

CD1, Track 34

1. Put students in pairs to say the sentences from Activity A.

2. Play the audio again, pausing for students to repeat the sentences with appropriate word stress.

3. Have students practice saying the sentences with their partners. Monitor and provide feedback on pronunciation.

C (10 minutes)

CD1, Track 35

1. Have students read the paragraph. Tell them to think about the content and the important information that is likely to be stressed.

2. Ask students to underline the words they expect to hear as stressed.

3. Put students in pairs to check their predictions.

4. Play the audio while students check their predictions. If necessary, pause to give students time to check.

5. Elicit the answers from volunteers. If there are any disagreements, play the audio again to confirm.

Activity C Answers, p. 57
You need to <u>experience</u> failure and <u>learn</u> from it, in order to <u>really</u> <u>succeed</u>. <u>Failing</u> is a <u>good</u> <u>preparation</u> for <u>life</u>. It makes you <u>stronger</u> and more able to <u>overcome</u> life's <u>problems</u>. <u>Don't</u> be <u>scared</u> of <u>failure</u>!

D (5 minutes)
 CD1, Track 36

1. Keep students in pairs. Play the audio again, pausing for students to repeat with appropriate word stress.

2. Have students practice reading the paragraph with their partners. Monitor and provide feedback on pronunciation.

For additional practice with stress on important words, have students visit *Q Online Practice*.

Speaking Skill: Asking for and giving clarification (5 minutes)

1. Direct students to read the information about asking for and giving clarification. Point out that it is always better to ask for clarification when one isn't sure.

2. Check comprehension: *Which phrases can be used to ask for clarification? Which phrases can be used to give clarification? Why is it a good idea to ask an audience for questions at the end of a presentation?*

3. Give students an opportunity to comment on other ways they know of to ask for or give clarification.

21ST CENTURY SKILLS

Developing critical thinking skills is essential to success in academics as well as the workplace. Being able to see both sides of an issue is one form of critical thinking. Help students develop proficiency in this skill through practice. Conduct "flash analysis" activities throughout whichever unit you are working on. Give students a statement, for example, in this unit, "Failure is more important than success." Ask students to list support for both sides of this statement. Randomly choose two students, one to say why this is true and the other to say why it is false. In order to reinforce the importance of seeing both sides of the issue, do not allow them to choose a position. Call on other students to supplement the reasons presented by the two students.

▶ *Listening and Speaking 3, page 58*

A (10 minutes)
 CD1, Track 37

1. Tell students they are going to listen to excerpts from a discussion. Have students read the excerpts from the conversation. Elicit any questions or difficulties.

2. Play the audio while students complete the conversations. Pause as necessary to give students time to write.

3. Put students in pairs to compare their answers. Call on volunteers to share their answers.

4. Play the audio again to clarify any difficulties.

5. Give pairs time to practice the conversations.

6. Call on volunteers to perform for the class.

Activity A Answers, p. 58
1. Sorry, I don't get what you mean;
2. What I'm trying to say is;
3. What do you mean exactly?
4. to give you an example;
5. Do you think you could say a bit more about that?
6. Can you give an example, please?

B (10 minutes)

1. Keep students in pairs. Explain that one student should read the statement and the other should ask for clarification. The student who read the statement should give clarification.

2. Point out that students should use what they remember from the listenings to help them give clarification.

3. Remind students to maintain eye contact and to link words with /j/ and /w/ where appropriate.

4. Monitor students' conversations for their use of phrases for asking for and giving clarification.

For additional practice with asking for and giving clarification, have students visit *Q Online Practice*.

▶ *Listening and Speaking 3, page 59*

ℚ Unit Assignment:
Take part in a pair discussion

Unit Question (5 minutes)

Refer students to the ideas they discussed at the beginning of the unit about the things we can learn from success and failure. Cue students if necessary by asking specific questions about the content of the unit: *Why do some people believe we can learn the same things from success and failure? Why do some people believe we learn more from failure than from success? Who are some of the people famous people we talked about who failed before becoming successful?*

Learning Outcome

1. Tie the unit assignment to the unit learning outcome. Say: *The outcome for this unit is to discuss successful and unsuccessful personal experiences and explain what you learned from them. This unit assignment is going to let you show your skill in participating in a discussion. Participating in a discussion is a useful skill because it allows people to share their experiences, viewpoints, and opinions. In doing so, we have the opportunity to educate and learn from others.*

2. Explain that you are going to use a rubric similar to their Self-Assessment checklist on page 62 to grade their unit assignment.

Consider the Ideas (10 minutes)

1. Tell students they are going to read some quotes by Albert Schweitzer, Winston Churchill, and Thomas Edison. Elicit what students know about these people.

2. Put students in groups to read the quotes and answer the questions.

3. Remind students to use the strategies for asking for and giving clarification if necessary.

4. Call on a reporter to share their group's information with the whole class.

> **Consider the Ideas Answers, p. 59**
> Answers will vary.

Consider the Ideas Background Note

Albert Schweitzer was a German philosopher, physician, and music scholar. He received the 1952 Nobel Peace Prize for his philosophical views that he put into action by establishing a hospital which is in the present-day African nation of Gabon.

Winston Churchill was the British Prime Minister during World War II. He was known for his gifted oratory skills and wartime leadership. He won the 1953 Nobel Prize for Literature for his writings on World War II.

Thomas Edison was an American inventor known for many inventions, including the phonograph, moving pictures (movies), and the light bulb.

Tip for Critical Thinking (1 minute)

Read the tip aloud. Point out that by paraphrasing, we can better remember and understand information, which makes it easier for us to convey it to others.

Critical Q: Expansion Activity

Paraphrasing

1. Tell students they are going to practice paraphrasing.

2. Tell students to look at the statements in the listen for main ideas activity on page 53. Have them paraphrase one or two of the statements.

3. Put students in pairs to share their paraphrases. Have them determine which of the statements their partner paraphrased. If students were unable to guess, have them point out the information that was missing or led them astray.

▶ *Listening and Speaking 3, page 60*

Prepare and Speak

Gather Ideas

A (10 minutes)

1. Direct students to read the questions and make their lists. Encourage them to list larger or important things as well as smaller, seemingly less important things. Remind them that they should list everything they can and not reject ideas at this stage.

▶ *Listening and Speaking 3, page 61*

Organize Ideas

B (10 minutes)

1. Remind students about the features of good notes. Elicit that we do not use complete sentences.

2. Have students choose an item from question 1 of Activity A to develop in Activity B. They should choose something for which they can answer all questions. Remind students to use notes instead of complete sentences.

3. Have students choose an item from question 2 of Activity A to develop in the second part of Activity B. Again, they should choose something for which they can answer all questions and they should use notes.

▶ *Listening and Speaking 3, page 62*

Speak

C (10–15 minutes)

1. Review the checklist on page 62. Ask students to read the checklist. Elicit any questions.

2. Put students in pairs to talk about their experiences. Remind them not to read directly from their outlines. Point out that the point of their discussion is to determine which experience taught the student more, the successful one or the failure.

3. Monitor students' performance as they work.

4. Use the unit assignment rubric on page 33 of this *Teacher's Handbook* to score each student's interview and answer.

5. Call on students you did not have a chance to monitor to present a summary of their discussion.

Alternative Unit Assignments

Assign or have students choose one of these assignments to do instead of, or in addition, to the unit assignment.

1. Think about three goals you have not achieved yet, but would like to. Discuss your ideas with a partner and explain what you will do to achieve these goals.

2. Some people like to "visualize" the goals they want to achieve. One way of doing this is to put up pictures of what they want, and focus on them each day. Do you think this can help you achieve your goals? Tell a partner why or why not.

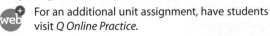 For an additional unit assignment, have students visit *Q Online Practice*.

Check and Reflect

Check

A (5 minutes)

1. Direct students to read and complete the Self-Assessment checklist.

2. Ask for a show of hands for how many students gave all or mostly yes answers.

3. Congratulate them on their success. Discuss the steps they can take if an item on the rubric was difficult for them. For example, if they had trouble using gerunds and infinitives as objects, they should review the rules more carefully and practice them on their own.

Reflect

B (5 minutes)

Refer students to the learning outcome on page 45. Tell them to talk with their partners about whether they achieved the learning outcome. Elicit the answers to the unit question that students came up with at the beginning of class. Encourage them to flip through the unit as they discuss the new things they learned and new answers they may have to the unit question.

▶ *Listening and Speaking 3, page 63*

Track Your Success

1. Have students circle the words they have learned in this unit. Suggest that students go back through the unit to review any words they have forgotten.

2. Have students check the skills they have mastered. If students need more practice to feel confident about their proficiency in a skill, point out the page numbers and encourage them to review.

3. Read the learning outcome aloud. Ask students if they feel that they have met the outcome.

Unit Assignment Rubric

Student name: _____

Date: _____

Unit Assignment: *Take part in a pair discussion.*

20 = Presentation element was completely successful (at least 90% of the time).
15 = Presentation element was mostly successful (at least 70% of the time).
10 = Presentation element was partially successful (at least 50% of the time).
 0 = Presentation element was not successful.

Take part in a pair discussion	20 points	15 points	10 points	0 points
Student spoke easily (without long pauses or reading) and was easy to understand (spoke clearly and at a good speed) while discussing successful and unsuccessful personal experiences.				
Student used appropriate word stress.				
Student correctly used gerunds and infinitives as objects.				
Student used vocabulary from the unit.				
Student was able to ask for and give clarification appropriately.				

Total points: _____

Comments:

Unit QUESTION

Is change good or bad?

New Perspectives

LISTENING • taking notes using a T-chart
VOCABULARY • using the dictionary
GRAMMAR • simple past and present perfect
PRONUNCIATION • variety of intonation to show interest
SPEAKING • asking for and giving reasons

LEARNING OUTCOME

Participate in a group discussion emphasizing the advantages and disadvantage of change.

▶ *Listening and* **Speaking 3, pages 64–65**

Preview the Unit

Learning Outcome

1. Ask for a volunteer to read the unit skills and then the unit learning outcome.

2. Explain: *The learning outcome is what you are expected to be able to do by the unit's end. You are going to be evaluated on how well you meet this outcome. With this in mind, you should focus on learning skills (Listening, Vocabulary, Grammar, Pronunciation, Speaking) that will support your goal of participating in a group discussion emphasizing the advantages and disadvantages of change. This can also help you act as mentors in the classroom to help the other students meet this outcome.*

A (10 minutes)

1. Prepare students for thinking about the topic by asking what changes students made in their lives to enter this institution. Share your own experiences about any changes you made in your life in order to teach this class.

2. Put students in pairs or small groups to discuss the first three questions.

3. Call on volunteers to share their ideas with the class. Ask questions to facilitate the discussion: *What has been the biggest change in your life? Were you happy about the change? Why or why not? Did you feel any other emotions, for example, fear, anger, confusion?*

4. Focus students' attention on the photo. Have a volunteer describe the photo to the class. Read the question aloud.

Activity A Answers, p. 65

1. Students may mention changes in their personal or professional lives, which may have affected them positively or negatively.

2. Students may wish to change nothing or a variety of personal or professional things.

3. The woman is moving her personal belongings. She probably feels the change is good because she's smiling.

B (15 minutes)

1. Introduce the Unit Question, "Is change good or bad?" Ask related information questions or questions about personal experience to help students prepare for answering the unit question, which is more abstract.

2. Read the Unit Question aloud. Give students a minute to silently consider their answer to the question. Say, *Let's consider the positive side of change in our individual lives. What are the good things about change? What are the disadvantages?*

3. Write *good* and *bad* at the top of two sheets of poster paper.

4. Elicit student answers and write them in the appropriate poster. Accept all contributions. Post the lists to refer to later in the unit.

Activity B Answers, p. 65
Possible answers: Change may be positive or negative, depending on the reasons for it as well as the way in which one copes with it; Change may be good or bad. It depends on why something changed and how we react to it; There are good changes in life and there are bad ones.

The Q Classroom

CD1, Track 38

1. Play *The Q Classroom*. Use the example from the audio to help students continue the conversation. Ask: *What types of change did the class discuss? Felix believes most changes have a good and a bad side. Do you agree with this statement? Why or why not?*

2. On the audio, Marcus and Yuna talk about starting their current course. Ask whether any of the students had similar experiences or feelings when coming to the institution they are currently studying at.

▶ *Listening and Speaking 3, page 66*

C (10 minutes)

1. Tell students they are going to answer a questionnaire about their opinions on change.

2. Have students complete their questionnaires individually. Tell students not to read the answer key yet.

Activity C Answers, p. 66
Students' answers will vary.

MULTILEVEL OPTION

Group lower-level students and assist them with the task. Ask higher-level students to predict what their answers say about their feelings toward change. Tell them to write a few lines justifying their answer.

D (10 minutes)

1. Ask students to read the answer key to determine what the questionnaire reveals about their attitude toward change.

2. Put students in groups to discuss their answers in Activity C and to answer the two questions in Activity D.

3. Choose a reporter to say whether the group members thought the questionnaire was accurate, and give the main reasons for their opinions.

4. Elicit any similarities or differences amongst the groups' answers.

Activity D Answers, p. 66
Students' answers may vary.

LISTENING

▶ *Listening and Speaking 3, page 67*

LISTENING 1: Changing Expectations

VOCABULARY (15 minutes)

1. Direct students to read the words and their definitions. Elicit any difficulties or questions.

2. Model correct pronunciation of the words. Say each word and have students repeat.

3. Ask students to complete the sentences.

4. Put students in pairs to check their answers. Ask volunteers to read their answers.

MULTILEVEL OPTION

Group lower-level students and assist them with the task. Point out the cues in the sentences that will help them to choose the correct word. Give them additional sentences to help them practice the difficult vocabulary. For example: *Our teacher always asks us to **justify** our opinions with examples. After college, I plan to look for an entry-level **position** in advertising.*

Have higher-level students complete the activity individually and then compare answers with a partner. Tell the pairs to write an additional sample sentence for each word. Have volunteers write one of their sentences on the board. Correct the sentences with the whole class, focusing on the use of the vocabulary word rather than other grammatical issues.

Vocabulary Answers, p. 67
1. crisis;   **2.** handle;   **3.** adapt;   **4.** curious;
5. steady;   **6.** fulfilled;   **7.** position;
8. considerably;   **9.** justify;   **10.** suffer

web⁺ For additional practice with the vocabulary, have students visit *Q Online Practice*.

▶ *Listening and Speaking 3, page 68*

PREVIEW LISTENING 1 (5 minutes)

1. Direct students to look at the photo. Ask: *Do you think the man looks fulfilled? Why or why not? What do you think his job is? Why?*

2. Read the introductory paragraph aloud. Have students check the reason they think Gary wanted to do something different. Tell students they should check their choice after the listening.

Preview the Listening Answers, p. 68
Students' answers will vary. The item mentioned in the listening is "He was curious about the world."

Listening 1 Background Note

The speaker talks about his career on Wall Street. Wall Street is a famous street in New York City. It is the heart of the city's financial district. The New York Stock Exchange is located on Wall Street, and many international banks have large offices there.

In contrast, Iowa is a state in the Midwest of the country. It is primarily farmland. Iowa, like all of the Midwest, is known for a more relaxed pace of life.

LISTEN FOR MAIN IDEAS (5 minutes)

CD1, Track 39

1. Ask students to read the sentences. Elicit any questions or difficulties about them.

2. Play the audio and have students choose their answers individually. Elicit the answers.

Main Idea Answers, p. 68
He changed his job; He moved home; He spent more time with his family; He found more friends.

▶ *Listening and Speaking 3, page 69*
LISTEN FOR DETAILS (10 minutes)

CD1, Track 40

1. Direct students to read the items before they listen again. Elicit any questions about them.

2. As you play the audio, have students listen and choose their answers.

3. Have students compare answers with a partner.

4. Replay the audio so that the partners can check their answers. Go over the answers with the class.

Listen for Details Answers, p. 69
1. a; **2.** b; **3.** a; **4.** a; **5.** b

 For additional practice with listening comprehension, have students visit *Q Online Practice.*

Q **WHAT DO YOU THINK?** (10 minutes)

1. Ask students to read the questions and reflect on their answers.

2. Seat students in small groups and assign roles: a group leader, a note-taker, a reporter, and a timekeeper.

3. Give students five minutes to discuss the questions. Call time if conversations are winding down. Allow them an extra minute or two if necessary.

4. Call on each group's reporter to share ideas with the class.

What Do You Think? Answers, p. 69
Students' answers may vary. Possible answers:
1. He learned that there are more important things in life than earning a lot of money. This will last because his family and friends are more important to him; This will not last because Gary will eventually want to have a lot of money again.
2. The sense of power and the ability to buy a lot of things.
3. Yes, because I am very flexible; No, because I would be used to having a lot of money and status.

Learning Outcome

Use the learning outcome to frame the purpose and relevance of Listening 1. Ask: *What did you learn from Listening 1 that prepares you to participate in a group discussion about the advantages and disadvantages of change? What did you learn that will help you to evaluate the effects of these changes?*

▶ *Listening and Speaking 3, page 70*
Listening Skill: Taking notes using a T-chart (10 minutes)

CD1, Track 41

1. Ask students to read the information about taking notes using a T-chart. Elicit any difficulties or questions.

2. Check comprehension by asking questions: *Why is a T-chart a useful tool for taking notes? What types of information are suitable for a T-chart format? Should you write complete sentences in the T-chart?*

3. Tell students they are going to listen to an excerpt about Gary's life as a city trader.

4. Play the audio while students study the advantages and disadvantages in the T-chart in their books.

A (10 minutes)

 CD1, Track 42

1. Tell students they are going to listen to a different excerpt from Gary's talk.

2. Copy the T-chart on the board. Elicit what the students remember about the advantages and disadvantages of being a home-care assistant. Write their answers in the appropriate place on the chart in note form.

3. Play the audio while students take notes in their books. If necessary, pause or play the audio again.

4. Call on a volunteer to give the answers. Compare the students' T-charts to that on the board. Suggest ways to improve the notes for clarity and brevity.

> **Activity A Answers, p. 70**
> Advantages: very fulfilled, slower pace of life, more friends, better relationship with family, healthier. Disadvantages: salary is lower, doesn't eat out often, can't buy a new car, can't afford an overseas vacation

Tip for Critical Thinking (1 minute)

Read the tip aloud. Point out that summarizing helps us to focus on the main points of something, which in turn helps us to retain information. Remind students that details are not included when we summarize because this makes it harder for us to remember the main points.

B (10 minutes)

1. Tell students to read the directions. Elicit any difficulties or questions.

2. Elicit some jobs that students can write about. Write them on the board.

3. Students take notes in their T-charts individually.

Critical Q: Expansion Activity

Summarizing

1. Tell students they are going to practice summarizing using a list instead of a T-chart by listening to "The Benefits of Failure" from Unit 3.
2. Write the title of the listening on the board as a list heading. Tell students to make a list in their notebooks. Explain that they should only write the main points from the listening, i.e., the benefits of failure.
3. Play track 26 of CD1 while students listen and make their lists.

4. Put students in pairs to compare their lists. Check by eliciting a class list. Remind students that a summary of main points should not include details.

C (10 minutes)

1. Read the directions aloud. Remind students not to tell their partner the name of the job.

2. Put students in pairs to describe the jobs they wrote about. Call on several students to share their descriptions with the class.

 For additional practice with taking notes using a T-chart, have students visit *Q Online Practice*.

▶ *Listening and Speaking 3, page 71*

LISTENING 2:
An Interview with Barbara Ehrenreich

VOCABULARY (10 minutes)

1. Model the pronunciation of the words in bold.

2. Put students in pairs to circle the answers. Call on volunteers to read the answers aloud.

> **Vocabulary Answers, p. 71**
> **1.** a; **2.** c; **3.** b; **4.** c; **5.** a;
> **6.** c; **7.** b; **8.** a; **9.** a; **10.** b

For additional practice with the vocabulary, have students visit *Q Online Practice*.

▶ *Listening and Speaking 3, page 72*

PREVIEW LISTENING 2 (5 minutes)

Read the background information to students. Elicit the reasons why a journalist might "go undercover" to do research. Write the answers on the board in note form. Tell students they will refer to the list once they have heard the interview.

Listening 2 Background Note

Barbara Ehrenreich was born in the United States in 1941. She has been interested in workers' rights across all sectors of the workforce since the 1960s. To date, she has written over 20 nonfiction books as well as one work of fiction and dozens of magazine articles and newspaper columns.

LISTEN FOR MAIN IDEAS (5 minutes)

CD1, Track 43

1. Ask students to read the statements. Elicit any difficulties with vocabulary or concepts.

2. Play the audio and have students work individually and write *T* or *F*.

> **Listen for Main Idea Answers, p. 72**
> **1.** T; **2.** F; **3.** T; **4.** F; **5.** T; **6.** F

▶ *Listening and Speaking 3, page 73*

LISTEN FOR DETAILS (5 minutes)

CD1, Track 44

1. Tell students they are going to listen again. Play the audio while students choose their answers individually.

2. Have students compare answers with a partner.

3. Go over the answers with the class.

> **Listen for Details Answers, p. 73**
> **1.** a; **2.** c; **3.** c; **4.** a; **5.** b; **6.** a; **7.** c; **8.** b

 For additional practice with listening comprehension, have students visit *Q Online Practice*.

▶ *Listening and Speaking 3, page 74*

WHAT DO YOU THINK?

A (10 minutes)

1. Ask students to read the questions and reflect on their answers.

2. Seat students in small groups and assign roles: a group leader, a note-taker, a reporter, and a timekeeper.

3. Give students five minutes to discuss the questions. Call time if conversations are winding down. Allow them an extra minute or two if necessary.

4. Call on each group's reporter to share ideas with the class.

> **Activity A Answers, p. 74**
> Students' answers will vary.
> **1.** It exposed a lot of truths about low-paying jobs that people did not know.
> **2.** A person needs to be able to completely change his or her lifestyle. I would not like to do this because I don't like change; I would like to do this because it would be very interesting.

B (10 minutes)

1. Have students continue working in their small groups. Tell them to choose a new leader, recorder, reporter, and timekeeper.

2. For question 1, encourage students to refer to their T-charts from Listening 1.

3. Call on the new reporter to share the group's answers to the questions.

> **Activity B Answers, p. 74**
> Possible Answers:
> Similarities: Both Gary and Barbara experienced dramatic changes in their lives.
> Differences: Gary learned a lot about himself, Barbara learned a lot about other people. Gary's life improved, Barbara's life became harder.

Tip for Success (1 minute)

Read the tip aloud. Point out that this tip is related to another tip students learned—making eye contact. Both of these behaviors show the speaker that we are paying attention to them.

Learning Outcome

Use the learning outcome to frame the purpose and relevance of Listenings 1 and 2 and the Critical Q activity of summarizing. Ask: *What did you learn from the listenings and Critical Q activity that prepares you to discuss the advantages and disadvantages of change?*

Vocabulary Skill: Using the dictionary (5 minutes)

1. Direct students to read the information silently.

2. Check comprehension: *Which word goes in the middle circle of the word web? Why? What is the purpose of the shortcut words? Does the word web contain only one part of speech?*

Skill Note

Remind students that the first definition of a word is the most common meaning and usage of that word.

Remind students that a dictionary also provides other useful information about a word, for example part of speech, irregular forms, and pronunciation.

▶ *Listening and Speaking 3, page 75*

A (5 minutes)

1. Put students in pairs or small groups to complete the activity.

2. Go over the answers with the class.

> **Activity A Answers, p. 75**
> **1.** become/make different   **2.** replace;
> **3.** bus/train/plane;   **4.** clothes;   **5.** money

B (5 minutes)

Have students build a word web with their partners. Call a volunteer to the front to complete a word web on the board.

> **MULTILEVEL OPTION**
>
> Group and assist lower-level students with the task. Have higher-level students look up additional words, for example, *break, set, fire,* and *do.*

 For additional practice with using the dictionary, have students visit *Q Online Practice.*

▶ *Listening and Speaking 3 page 76*

SPEAKING

Grammar: Simple past and present perfect (10 minutes)

1. Read the information about the simple past and present perfect.

2. Check comprehension by asking questions: *Which verb form do we use for events that are no longer happening? Which verb form do we use* since *and* for *with?*

3. Review the past participle forms needed for the past perfect. Elicit some of the irregular past participle forms, e.g., *written, seen, ridden, taken.*

4. Remind students that time expressions are frequently used with these verb forms. Elicit some common phrases using *last, ago, in,* and *on.* Repeat with *since* and *for.*

▶ *Listening and Speaking 3, page 77*

A (15 minutes)

1. Tell students to circle the correct verb forms individually. Remind them to look at the grammar note for help.

2. Put students in pairs to check their answers. Check the answers as a class.

3. Have students practice the conversation.

> **Activity A Answers, p. 77**
> **1.** Have you ever traveled;   **2.** I have;
> **3.** went;   **4.** Did you enjoy;   **5.** was;
> **6.** haven't been;   **7.** traveled

B (5 minutes)

Have students work individually to make their list. Encourage students to choose events that are clear to them.

> **Activity B Answers, p. 77**
> Students' answers will vary. Students should correctly use the simple past.

C (5 minutes)

Have students work individually to make their list.

> **Activity C Answers, p. 77**
> Students' answers will vary. Students should correctly use the present perfect.

D (10 minutes)

1. Put students in groups to discuss their lists.

2. Encourage them to use the simple past for events that happened during their childhood. Encourage them to use present perfect for events that have happened since their childhood.

3. Have a reporter share some of the group's events.

 For additional practice with the simple past and present perfect, have students visit *Q Online Practice.*

▶ *Listening and Speaking 3, page 78*

Pronunciation: Variety of intonation to show interest (15 minutes)

 CD1, Track 45

1. Read the information about varying intonation.

2. Check comprehension by asking: *What does rising intonation mean? What does falling intonation mean? Why is intonation important?*

3. Tell students to listen to the audio. Elicit what they notice about the second time the speaker says the sentence. Write the sentence on the board. Draw an arrow over the words to show the rising and falling intonation.

4. Tell students they are going to listen to some more examples. Have them draw the intonation changes over the sentences as they read along.

5. Play the audio as students write the intonation changes. Copy the sentences on the board and elicit the intonation changes.

A (10 minutes)
 CD1, Track 46

1. Play the audio. Tell students to check which speaker sounds more interested.

2. Elicit the answers from volunteers. If there are any disagreements, play the audio again to confirm.

> **Activity A Answers, p. 78**
> **1.** Speaker 2; **2.** Speaker 1;
> **3.** Speaker 2; **4.** Speaker 2;
> **5.** Speaker 1; **6.** Speaker 1;
> **7.** Speaker 2; **8.** Speaker 1

B (5 minutes)
CD1, Track 47

Play the audio again, pausing for students to repeat the sentences with appropriate intonation.

 For additional practice with intonation to show interest, have students visit *Q Online Practice*.

Expansion Activity: Intonation in job interviews
(15 minutes)

1. Pair students. Remind them that proper intonation is very useful in job interviews and other situations when they want to make a good first impression.

2. Tell students that they are going to practice varying their intonation to show interest while role-playing a job interview.

3. Assign roles. One student should be the interviewer, the other the potential employee.

4. Throughout the conversation, the interviewer should state facts about his or her "company." The potential employee should respond with appropriate intonation.

5. Ask volunteers to repeat their conversation for the class.

▶ *Listening and Speaking 3, page 79*

Speaking Skill: Asking for and giving reasons (5 minutes)

CD1, Track 48

1. Direct students to read the information about asking for and giving reasons. Point out that others expect us to give reasons for our opinions.

2. Check comprehension: *Which phrases can be used to ask for reasons? Which phrases can be used to give reasons? Why do we ask for reasons?*

3. Tell student they are going to listen to the way in which these phrases are used in conversation.

4. Play the audio while students read the conversation.

21ST CENTURY SKILLS

Appropriate intonation is essential to communicating effectively in one's professional and academic life. The wrong intonation can create misunderstandings. Help students to develop intonation awareness by saying *hello* in the following ways: annoyed, interested, and questioning. Ask students to describe your intonation. Have students repeat *hello* using each intonation. Put students in pairs to practice saying the following sentences in the three ways: 1. *How are you?* 2. *I love English.* 3. *Change is good.* Have their partner guess which feeling they are conveying when the say the sentence. Have volunteers perform for the class.

A (10 minutes)
CD1, Track 49

1. Tell students they are going to listen to a conversation between friends. Have them read the excerpts. Elicit any questions or difficulties.

2. Play the audio while students complete the conversations. Pause as necessary.

3. Put students in pairs to compare their answers. Call on volunteers to share their answers.

4. Give pairs time to practice the conversations. Call on volunteers to perform for the class.

> **Activity A Answers, p. 79**
> **1.** Why do you say that? **2.** Because,
> **3.** first of all, **4.** Another reason is, **5.** also

Tip for Success (1 minute)

Read the tip aloud. Point out that asking questions is a useful way to keep a conversation going. Ask students to look at the conversation in Activity A and find the expressions and questions that keep the conversation going.

▶ *Listening and Speaking 3, page 80*

B (10 minutes)

1. Ask students to read the activities in the box. Elicit the meaning of each activity. Tell students to write an item of their own in the space provided.

2. Put students in groups to discuss the activities they'd like to try. Remind them of turn-taking strategies. Elicit some phrases to use when signaling another's turn, e.g., *How about you?*

3. Remind students to maintain eye contact, to link words, and to use questions to keep the conversation going.

4. Monitor students' conversations for their use of phrases for asking for and giving reasons.

 For additional practice with asking for and giving reasons, have students visit *Q Online Practice*.

Unit Assignment:
Take part in a group discussion

Unit Question (5 minutes)

Refer students to the ideas they discussed at the beginning of the unit about the good and bad aspects of change. Cue students if necessary by asking specific questions about the content of the unit: *What are some of the feelings that people we've talked about have had about change in their lives? Can you give examples? What are some of the types of change we've talked about?*

Learning Outcome

1. Tie the unit assignment to the unit learning outcome. Say: *The outcome for this unit is to discuss the advantages and disadvantages of change. This unit assignment is going to let you show your skill in participating in a discussion. Participating in a discussion is a useful skill because it allows people to share their experiences, viewpoints, and opinions. In doing so, we have the opportunity to educate and learn from others.*

2. Explain that you are going to use a rubric similar to their Self-Assessment checklist on page 82 to grade their unit assignment.

Consider the Ideas (10 minutes)

1. Tell students they are going to discuss the advantages and disadvantages of several important events that can occur in one's life.

2. Put students in groups to discuss the events. Tell them to choose a group reporter.

3. Remind students to use the strategies for asking for and giving reasons.

4. Call on reporters to share their group's information on one of the events with the whole class.

> **Consider the Ideas Answers, p. 80**
> Answers will vary. Students should be able to discuss advantages and disadvantages for each event while using phrases from the speaking skill.

▶ *Listening and Speaking 3, page 81*

Prepare and Speak

Gather Ideas

A (5 minutes)

Direct students to read the questions and choose an event that they have experienced. If they have experienced more than one event, tell them to choose the event that has changed their life the most or that they remember most clearly.

Organize Ideas

B (10 minutes)

1. Remind students that they do not have to use complete sentences or words when they write something in notes.

2. Have students make a T-chart to list the advantages and disadvantages that resulted from the change from Activity A.

3. Tell students to summarize their findings in one or two main points that they have learned as a result.

Speak

C (10–15 minutes)

1. Ask students to review the Self-Assessment checklist on page 82. Elicit any questions.

2. Put students in groups to talk about their experiences. Remind them not to read directly from their outlines or T-charts.

3. Tell students to make a T-chart to take notes during each group member's part of the discussion.

4. Monitor students' performance as they work.

5. Call on students you did not have a chance to monitor to present a summary of their discussion.

6. Use the Unit Assignment Rubric on page 43 of this *Teacher's Handbook* to score each student's interview and answer.

Tip for Success (1 minute)

Read the tip aloud. Point out that taking notes is useful to help you remember the main points when many people are participating in a discussion.

Alternative Unit Assignments

Assign or have students choose one of these assignments to do instead of, or in addition, to the unit assignment.

1. Do you agree that travel changes your ideas, and gives you a better understanding of people and places? Give reasons for your ideas and ask your partner for his or her reasons.

2. Losing your job can cause big changes. Read the roles and then role-play the conversation in pairs:

Student A: You have lost your job. You really liked it, and now you feel depressed. Tell your partner what job you had, and why you liked it. Explain how losing your job has changed your life.

Student B: Listen to your partner. Show sympathy, and encourage your partner to be positive. Think of ways in which this change might be a good thing. Can you persuade your partner to see things differently?

 For an additional Unit Assignment, have students visit *Q Online Practice.*

Check and Reflect

Check

A (5 minutes)

1. Direct students to read and complete the Self-Assessment checklist.

2. Ask for a show of hands for how many students gave all or mostly yes answers.

3. Congratulate them on their success. Discuss the steps they can take if an item on the rubric was difficult for them. For example, if they had trouble using the simple past and present perfect, they should review the rules more carefully.

Reflect

B (5 minutes)

Refer students to the learning outcome on page 65. Tell them to talk with their partners about whether they achieved the learning outcome. Elicit the answers to the unit question that students came up with at the beginning of class. Encourage them to flip through the unit as they discuss the new things they learned and new answers they may have to the unit question.

▶ *Listening and Speaking 3, page 83*

Track Your Success

1. Have students circle the words they have learned in this unit. Suggest that students go back through the unit to review any words they have forgotten.

2. Have students check the skills they have mastered. If students need more practice to feel confident about their proficiency in a skill, point out the page numbers and encourage them to review.

3. Read the learning outcome aloud. Ask students if they feel that they have met the outcome.

Unit Assignment Rubric

Student name: _____

Date: _____

Unit Assignment: *Take part in a group discussion.*

20 = Presentation element was completely successful (at least 90% of the time).
15 = Presentation element was mostly successful (at least 70% of the time).
10 = Presentation element was partially successful (at least 50% of the time).
 0 = Presentation element was not successful.

Take part in a group discussion	20 points	15 points	10 points	0 points
Student spoke easily about the advantages and disadvantages of change (without long pauses or reading) and was easy to understand (spoke clearly and at a good speed).				
Student used a variety of intonation.				
Student correctly used the simple past and present perfect.				
Student used vocabulary from the unit.				
Student was able to ask for and give reasons appropriately.				

Total points: _____

Comments:

Unit QUESTION

Are we responsible for the world we live in?

Responsibility

LISTENING • inferring a speaker's attitude

VOCABULARY • using the dictionary

GRAMMAR • tag questions

PRONUNCIATION • intonation in tag questions

SPEAKING • leading a group discussion

LEARNING OUTCOME

State and explain your opinions about our responsibility for issues impacting our world.

▶ *Listening and Speaking 3, pages 84–85*

Preview the Unit

Learning Outcome

1. Ask for a volunteer to read the unit skills and then the unit learning outcome.

2. Explain: *The learning outcome is what you are expected to be able to do by the unit's end. You are going to be evaluated on how well you meet this outcome. With this in mind, you should focus on learning skills (Listening, Vocabulary, Grammar, Pronunciation, Speaking) that will support your goal of stating and explaining your opinions about our responsibility for issues impacting the world. This can also help you act as mentors in the classroom to help the other students meet this outcome.*

A (10 minutes)

1. Prepare students for thinking about the topic by asking what *responsibility* means to the students. Elicit a class definition of *responsibility* and write it on the board to refer to later. Accept all contributions.

2. Put students in pairs or small groups to discuss the first two questions.

3. Call on volunteers to share their ideas with the class. Ask questions to facilitate the discussion: *What does it mean to be a responsible citizen? Why do you think you are or are not a responsible citizen?*

4. Focus students' attention on the photo. Have a volunteer describe the photo to the class. Read the question aloud.

Activity A Answers, p. 85

1. Students' answers may depend on their definition of *responsibility*. Ask for reasons for their answer.

2. Students may say they are responsible because they help out in their community.

3. The man is looking in the turtle's mouth. He's showing responsibility toward the animal and nature because we have powerful effects over their habitats.

B (15 minutes)

1. Introduce the Unit Question, "Are we responsible for the world we live in?" Ask related information questions or questions about personal experience to help students prepare for answering the unit question, which is more abstract. *How can we define the world we live in? Does this mean our community? Our country? Our planet? All of the above? How much responsibility can one person have for his or her community, country, planet?*

2. Read the Unit Question aloud. Give students a minute to silently consider their answer to the question. Then ask students who would answer yes to stand on one side of the room and students who would answer no to stand on the other side of the room.

3. Direct students to tell a partner next to them their reason for choosing that side of the issue.

4. Call on volunteers from each side to share their opinions with the class.

5. After students have shared their opinions, provide an opportunity for anyone who would like to change sides to do so.

6. Ask students to sit down, copy the unit question, and make a note of their answers and their reasons. They will refer to these notes at the end of the unit.

Possible answers: Yes, we are responsible because we pollute the environment, and we have a responsibility to take care of it; Yes, we are responsible because we are the only ones who can do anything. Yes, we are responsible because the world needs help.

The Q Classroom
CD2, Track 02

1. Play *The Q Classroom.* Use the example from the audio to help students continue the conversation. Ask: *What three ways are mentioned as ways in which people can be responsible in their communities? Which of these three things do you do? Which don't you do? Why not?*

2. On the audio, the teacher asks if people should be responsible as individuals or if the government should take some responsibility for taking care of the community and environment. Elicit students' opinion on this issue. Ask them to support their opinions with examples.

▶ *Listening and Speaking 3, page 86*

C (10 minutes)

1. Tell students they are going to answer a survey on roles and responsibilities. Ask students to read the survey. Elicit any questions about vocabulary.

2. Put students in pairs to discuss who should be responsible for each activity. Explain that they should choose from the list of people on the right and that they can use a group more than once.

Activity C Answers, p. 86
Students' answers will vary.

MULTILEVEL OPTION

Group and assist lower-level students with the task. Ask higher-level students to brainstorm other community issues, for example, the maintenance of community green spaces and parks. Ask them to discuss who should be responsible for these additional activities.

D (10 minutes)

1. Put the pairs in groups to discuss their ideas and their reasons for assigning responsibilities as they did. Remind them to use their notes as a basis for their discussion, not as a list to simply read aloud.

2. Ask a reporter from each group to state which people should be responsible for each activity and why.

3. Ask groups to discuss how individual members feel or do not feel responsible for each activity. Remind groups to discuss examples of ways that the members take responsibility.

4. Choose a different student to report how the group members felt about being responsible for one of the activities, for example picking up litter. Encourage the reporter to give the best example of the way in which one of the group members takes responsibility for the activity.

Activity D Answers, p. 86
Students' answers will vary. Students should be able to give reasons and examples for their answers.

Expansion Activity: Other ways to take responsibility (10 minutes)

1. Seat students in groups or have them stay in their groups from Activity D.

2. Ask students to think of the things on the web survey that they currently do not take responsibility for, and write them down.

3. Students should then brainstorm ways they can take responsibility for these things and discuss these with their group.

4. Elicit ideas from the group.

LISTENING

▶ *Listening and Speaking 3, page 87*

LISTENING 1:
Corporate Social Responsibility

VOCABULARY (15 minutes)

1. Direct students to read the words and their definitions. Elicit any difficulties or questions.

2. Model correct pronunciation of the words. Say each word and have students repeat.

3. Ask students to complete the sentences.

4. Put students in pairs to check answers. Elicit answers. Correct as necessary.

Group lower-level students and assist them with the task. Point out the cues in the sentences that will help them to choose the correct word. Give them additional sentences to help them practice the difficult vocabulary. For example: *The actions of humans have a powerful **impact** on the natural world; It isn't polite to **demand** attention from your teacher when other students are ahead of you.*

Have higher-level students complete the activity individually and then compare answers in pairs. Tell the pairs to write another sample sentence for each word. Have volunteers write one of their sentences on the board. Check the sentences as a class, focusing on the use of vocabulary rather than grammatical issues.

Vocabulary Answers, p. 87
1. consumer; **2.** fair; **3.** ignore;
4. fine; **5.** profit; **6.** benefit;
7. demand; **8.** pollute; **9.** impact;
10. Developed

 For additional practice with the vocabulary, have students visit *Q Online Practice*.

▶ *Listening and Speaking 3, page 88*
PREVIEW LISTENING 1 (5 minutes)

1. Direct students to look at the photo. Ask: *In which ways are clothing companies responsible for people or the environment? How might a clothing company take advantage of its workers?*

2. Read the introductory paragraph aloud. Brainstorm the meaning of "corporate social responsibility" as a class. Write the class definition of it on the board.

Preview Listening 1 Answers, p. 88
Students' answers will vary. In the listening, the term is defined as the need for companies to be responsible for the economic, social, and environmental impact of their actions.

Listening 1 Background Note

The professor mentions the use of children in the production of clothing. These children work in what is typically called a sweatshop. A sweatshop is a manufacturing operation that underpays employees— often women and underage workers—and asks them to work long hours. The working conditions may be particularly difficult or unsafe. The workers are not protected and are often taken advantage of. Sweatshops exist throughout the world, but they are illegal in most countries.

The professor also mentions the corporate movement that dates back to the 19th century in Britain. At that time, working conditions were not good and workers had few rights. As a result, there was a movement to organize workers into unions so that they could find protection or solidarity as a group.

LISTEN FOR MAIN IDEAS (5 minutes)

 CD2, Track 03

Ask students to read the sentences. Elicit any questions or difficulties. Play the audio and have students choose their answers individually. Elicit the answers.

Main Idea Answers, p. 88
1. T; **2.** F; **3.** F; **4.** T; **5.** T; **6.** F

▶ *Listening and Speaking 3, page 89*
LISTEN FOR DETAILS (10 minutes)

 CD2, Track 04

1. Direct students to read the items before they listen again. Elicit any questions about them.

2. As you play the audio, have students listen and choose their answers.

3. Have students compare answers with a partner.

4. Replay the audio so that the partners can check their answers.

5. Go over the answers with the class.

Listen for Details Answers, p. 89
1. a; **2.** a; **3.** b; **4.** a; **5.** b

 For additional practice with listening comprehension, have students visit *Q Online Practice*.

Tip for Success (1 minute)

Read the tip aloud. Point out that students may want to review the vocabulary words before they begin their discussions.

 WHAT DO YOU THINK? (10 minutes)

1. Ask students to read the questions and reflect on their answers.

2. Seat students in small groups and assign roles: a group leader, a note-taker, a reporter, and a timekeeper.

3. Give students five minutes to discuss the questions. Call time if conversations are winding down. Allow them an extra minute or two if necessary.

4. Call on each group's reporter to share ideas with the class.

> **What Do You Think? Answers, p. 89**
> Answers will vary. Possible answers:
> **1.** It is very important. The benefits are the people respect the companies more and might buy more things from them because of it.
> **2.** The company is because it is more powerful; Individuals are because change has to start with an individual person's decisions.
> **3.** Student may talk about companies in their own country.

Learning Outcome

Use the learning outcome to frame the purpose and relevance of Listening 1. Ask: *What did you learn from Listening 1 that prepares you to state and explain your opinions about our responsibility for issues impacting our world? What did you learn that will help you to identify these issues?*

▶ *Listening and Speaking 3, page 90*

Listening Skill: Inferring a speaker's attitude (15 minutes)

CD2, Track 05

1. Ask students to read the information about inferring a speaker's attitude. Elicit any difficulties or questions.

2. Check comprehension by asking questions: *Why might someone speak slowly or hesitate before speaking? Why might someone raise his or her voice when speaking? What are the speaking characteristics of someone who is bored or uninterested?*

3. Elicit how these speech characteristics are the same or different from their own languages.

4. Tell students they are going to listen to an excerpt from the lecture in which the professor feels a little angry. Ask them to read along and mark where the professor raises his voice or sounds angry. Elicit from students the words for which the professor raises his voice.

5. Tell students they are going to listen to a conversation in which Speaker A is bored and Speaker B is nervous. Ask them to read along and mark the point of hesitation in Speaker B's speech.

6. Play the audio while students read along. Elicit the place where Speaker B hesitates.

A (5 minutes)
CD2, Track 06

1. Tell students they are going to listen to three sentences and match them with the speaker's attitude.

2. Play the audio while students match. If necessary, pause or play the audio again.

3. Check the answers as a class.

> **Activity A Answers, p. 90**
> **1.** nervous; **2.** angry; **3.** uninterested

B (10 minutes)
CD2, Track 07

1. Tell students they are going to listen to three conversations. Tell them to check the word that describes the way the woman in the conversation feels.

2. Review quickly the features of each attitude by eliciting the characteristics of speech for that attitude.

3. Play the audio while students check the words.

4. Call on volunteers to read their answers.

> **Activity B Answers, p. 90**
> **1.** angry; **2.** uninterested; **3.** nervous

C (5 minutes)

1. Read the directions to the students. Ask students to read the sentences quickly. Elicit any difficulties or questions about vocabulary.

2. Put students in pairs. Tell them to think of a situation for each sentence in which it would be said nervously, angrily, or with no interest. Explain that this will help them to do the activity.

3. Have students practice the sentences with their partners. Call on a volunteer to read the sentence angrily. Call on different volunteers to read the other two sentences in the different ways.

 For additional practice with inferring a speaker's attitude, have students visit *Q Online Practice*.

▶ *Listening and Speaking 3, page 91*

LISTENING 2: Personal Responsibility

VOCABULARY (10 minutes)

1. Model the pronunciation of the words in bold.

2. Put students in pairs to write the words or phrases next to the correct definitions. Call on volunteers to read the answers aloud.

Vocabulary Answers, p. 91

a. check up on; **b.** trust; **c.** guilty;
d. sensible; **e.** influence; **f.** obligation;
g. lie; **h.** in charge of; **i.** help out;
j. appropriate

 For additional practice with the vocabulary, have students visit *Q Online Practice*.

▶ *Listening and Speaking 3, page 92*

PREVIEW LISTENING 2 (5 minutes)

1. Direct students' attention to the photo and ask: *Do you drink bottled water? If yes, what do you do with the bottles? If no, what do you think people who do drink bottled water should do with the bottles? Why?*

2. Read the paragraph aloud. Ask students to brainstorm a list of things they are personally responsible for during the day. Tell them to include things as small as recycling water bottles.

Listening 2 Background Note

Many young people live at home while they are going to college or a university. They do this to save money. Most young people are expected to contribute to the household chores, for example, doing dishes, keeping the house clean, or helping with meals. Similarly, teenagers who are still in high school usually live at home. They may be responsible for taking care of younger children in the household in addition to helping with chores.

LISTEN FOR MAIN IDEAS (5 minutes)

CD2, Track 8

1. Ask students to read the statements. Elicit any difficulties with vocabulary or concepts.

2. Play the audio and have students work individually to choose the correct answer. Check as a class.

Listen for Main Idea Answers, p. 92
1. a; **2.** b; **3.** a; **4.** c; **5.** b

LISTEN FOR DETAILS (10 minutes)

CD2, Track 9

1. Tell students they are going to listen again. Play the audio while students match the responsibilities and the students.

2. Have students compare answers with a partner.

3. Go over the answers with the class. Elicit what each person from the listening does.

Listen for Details Answers, p. 92
1. c; **2.** a; **3.** c; **4.** b; **5.** b; **6.** d

 For additional practice with listening comprehension, have students visit *Q Online Practice*.

▶ *Listening and Speaking 3, page 93*

WHAT DO YOU THINK?

A (10 minutes)

1. Ask students to read the questions and reflect on their answers.

2. Seat students in small groups and assign roles: a group leader, a note-taker, a reporter, and a timekeeper.

3. Give students five minutes to discuss the questions. Call time if conversations are winding down. Allow them an extra minute or two if necessary.

4. Call on each group's reporter to share ideas with the class.

Activity A Answers, p. 93
Students' answers will vary. Possible answers:
1. My family gives me a lot of responsibility because I'm the oldest. Sometimes I wish I had less responsibility!
2. I think it depends on the person. Some people mature more quickly than others.

B (10 minutes)

1. Have students continue working their small groups to discuss the questions in Activity B. Tell them to choose a new leader, recorder, reporter, and timekeeper.

2. For question 1, encourage students to refer to the pages in their book for Listening 1.

3. Call on the new reporter to share the group's answers to the questions.

Activity B Answers, p. 93
Students' answers will vary. Possible answers:
1. Companies should be careful not to pollute and to follow environmental laws. Individuals should recycle and reduce waste.
2. By recycling, by walking instead of driving, by reducing waste.

Learning Outcome

Use the learning outcome to frame the purpose and relevance of Listenings 1 and 2 Ask: *What did you learn from Listening 1 and 2 that prepares you to form an opinion about our responsibility for issues impacting our world? What did you learn that will help you express them?*

Vocabulary Skill: Using the dictionary (10 minutes)

1. Direct students to read the information silently.

2. Check comprehension: *What is the first thing you should identify to help you find the correct meaning of a word? What should you do after this? What is the* context *of a word?*

3. Ask students to read the conversation to determine the part of speech for the word *wrong*. Then ask them to read the paragraph after the conversation to check their answer.

4. Tell students to read the definitions to find out why definition number 4 is correct. Elicit any questions or difficulties about the entry.

Skill Note

Point out that the dictionary often lists words or phrases that are common with a particular word. Explain that these are commonly called collocations. These are words and phrases that typically go together in a particular context or situation. Point out that when the words are in parentheses it means that they are not required but they may frequently be used with the word to express that meaning. Elicit the collocation for definition number 4 of the word *wrong*.

> **MULTILEVEL OPTION**
>
> Group lower-level students and assist them with finding the collocations for the word *wrong* in definitions number 3 and 4. Ask higher-level students to write a sentence using the collocations for the word *wrong* as listed in definitions number 3 and 4.

▶ *Listening and Speaking 3, page 94*

A (15 minutes)

1. Put students in pairs or small groups to complete the activity.

2. Go over the answers with the class.

Activity A Answers, p. 94

2. (noun) the highest level
3. (verb) to stop doing something without achieving what you wanted to do
4. (adj) not yet paid or done
5. (verb) to use something in a bad or dishonest way
6. (adj) having high standards of behavior
7. (verb) take the chance that something bad will happen
8. (adj) honest and willing to talk

B (10 minutes)

1. Keep students in pairs, but have students write their sentences individually.

2. Have students compare their sentences with the partner. Call on volunteers to share one sentence.

Activity B Answers, p. 94

Students' answers will vary. Sample sentences include:

1. It is important not to **risk** the environment for profit.
2. It is not **just** to pay workers less than a fair wage.
3. People won't like a politician if he or she **abuses** power.
4. People and companies should be **moral** in their actions.
5. You must pay your **outstanding** library fines or you won't be allowed to register for next term.

 For additional practice with using the dictionary, have students visit *Q Online Practice*.

▶ *Listening and Speaking 3, page 95*

SPEAKING

Grammar: Tag questions (10 minutes)

1. Read aloud the information about tag questions.

2. Check comprehension by asking questions: *If the statement is positive, should the tag question be positive or negative? If the statement is negative, should the tag question be positive or negative? What is the subject of a tag question? What should we do if the statement contains an auxiliary verb or modal? When should we use* do *in the tag question?*

Skill Note

Review the question tag forms of the simple present, simple past, present continuous, past continuous, and present perfect. For example:

She was here, wasn't she? We weren't there, were we?

He was living here, wasn't he? They weren't living there, were they?

Elicit the main verb and auxiliary verbs for each statement and question tag.

A (10 minutes)

1. Tell students to complete the tag questions individually.

2. Remind them to look at the grammar note for help.

3. Put students in pairs to check their answers. Check the answers as a class.

4. Have students practice the conversation.

> **Activity A Answers, p. 95**
> **1.** aren't you?   **2.** does he?   **3.** did they?
> **4.** isn't it?   **5.** shouldn't she?   **6.** have they?
> **7.** didn't she?   **8.** can we?

▶ *Listening and Speaking 3, page 96*

B (5 minutes)

1. Keep students in pairs, but have them work individually to complete the activity.

2. Encourage students to use vocabulary or themes from the unit.

> **Activity B Answers, p. 96**
> **1.** have you?
> **2.** shouldn't they?
> Answers will vary. Possible answers:
> **3.** We need to recycle, don't we?
> **4.** He was taking care of his sister, wasn't he?
> **5.** The company hasn't polluted the river, has it?

C (5 minutes)

Have students take turns asking and answering the questions from Activity B. Call on several volunteers to share their original sentences and answers with the class.

 For additional practice with tag questions, have students visit *Q Online Practice*.

▶ *Listening and Speaking 3, page 97*

Pronunciation:
Intonation in tag questions (10 minutes)

CD2, Track 10

1. Read the information about intonation in tag questions.

2. Check comprehension by asking: *When do we use rising intonation in the tag question? When do we use falling intonation in the tag question?*

3. Tell students to read the sentence while they listen to the audio. Have them run their fingers along the arrows as they listen.

4. Play the audio again as a model for the students. Stop for students to repeat the sentences with correct intonation.

A (10 minutes)
CD2, Track 11

1. Have students read the sentences.

2. Tell students they will check whether the sentence has rising or falling intonation. Encourage them to write intonation arrows above the sentences as they listen.

3. Play the audio while students write their arrows and check their answers.

4. Elicit the answers from volunteers. If there are any disagreements, play the audio again to confirm.

> **Activity A Answers, p. 97**
> **1.** Rise;   **2.** Rise;   **3.** Fall;   **4.** Fall

B (5 minutes)
CD2, Track 12

1. Tell students that they are going to use what they know about question intonation to determine whether or not the speaker knows the answer to the question.

2. Elicit the meaning of rising and falling intonation from the class.

3. Play the audio while students check their answers. Encourage them to draw arrows above the sentences to show the intonation pattern.

> **Activity B Answers, p. 97**
> **1.** Rise, knows the answer;   **2.** Fall, doesn't know;
> **3.** Rise, knows;   **4.** Fall, doesn't know

▶ *Listening and Speaking 3, page 98*

C (5 minutes)
CD2, Tracks 11 and 12

Play the audio, pausing for students to repeat the sentences with appropriate intonation. Have students repeat the sentences chorally and individually.

D (5 minutes)

1. Put students in pairs. Tell them to take turns reading the sentences from Activities A and B.

2. Have their partners draw another arrow above each sentence to show whether the intonation they hear is rising or falling.

 For additional practice with intonation in tag questions, have students visit *Q Online Practice*.

Speaking Skill:
Leading a group discussion (5 minutes)

1. Direct students to read the information about leading a group discussion. Point out that an effective discussion typically needs a leader to guide the flow.

2. Check comprehension: *What are some of the things the discussion leader is responsible for? What are the phrases he or she can use to start the discussion? What about to end it?*

21ST CENTURY SKILLS

Debating is something students may need to do in their professional lives as well as their academic lives. To debate well, students must be able to identify a variety of viewpoints or arguments and plan responses to them accordingly. Help students develop comfort with this important skill through extensive practice. Conduct "short debate" activities throughout whichever unit you are working on. (This will often help them prepare for the unit assignment as well.) Assign a very specific topic, for example, in this unit, "Responsibility for the cleanliness of our school." Give students three minutes to think of all the reasons why they should and should not be responsible for this. Then put the students in two groups and assign the viewpoint that their group should defend. Seat the students in rows across from each other and have them debate the points for and against responsibility for cleanliness of the school. If your class is large, select two groups of students to debate and the others to observe and determine which side made a more convincing argument.

▶ *Listening and Speaking 3, page 99*

A (10 minutes)

◄)) CD2, Track 13

1. Tell students they are going to listen to an excerpt from a discussion on recycling. Have students read the excerpt. Elicit any questions or difficulties.

2. Play the audio while students complete the conversation. Pause as necessary.

3. Put students in groups to compare their answers. Call on volunteers to share their answers.

4. Play the audio again to clarify any difficulties.

5. Give groups time to practice the conversations. Call on volunteers to perform for the class.

> **Activity A Answers, p. 99**
> **1.** we're going to look at; **2.** what's your opinion;
> **3.** What do you think; **4.** can we keep to the topic;
> **5.** Do you have anything to add; **6.** to sum up, then

B (10 minutes)

1. Split the groups into pairs. Tell the pairs to continue the discussion using their own ideas.

2. Remind them that they are no longer leading a discussion since they are in a pair. Elicit some of the things they should do when discussing with a partner, for example, maintain eye contact, give reasons, take turns, etc.

3. Monitor students' conversations for their use of phrases for asking for and giving reasons and taking turns.

 For additional practice with leading a group discussion, have students visit *Q Online Practice*.

▶ *Listening and Speaking 3, page 100*

Unit Assignment:
Take part in a group discussion

Unit Question (5 minutes)

Refer students to the ideas they discussed at the beginning of the unit about whether we are responsible for the world we live in. Cue students if necessary by asking specific questions about the content of the unit: *What are the types of responsibility we talked about? What is corporate social responsibility? What are some the things we are responsible for as individuals?*

Learning Outcome

1. Tie the unit assignment to the unit learning outcome. Say: *The outcome for this unit is to discuss whether we are responsible for the world we live in. This unit assignment is going to let you show your skill in participating in a discussion. Participating in a discussion is a useful skill because it allows people to share their experiences, viewpoints, and opinion. In doing so, we have the opportunity to educate and learn from others.*

2. Explain that you are going to use a rubric similar to their Self-Assessment checklist on page 102 to grade their unit assignment.

Consider the Ideas (5 minutes)

1. Tell students they are going to brainstorm a list of issues that affect their world. Elicit the examples given in book.

2. Put students in groups to brainstorm a list. Depending on the size of your class, you may want to assign a category to each group.

3. Remind students that when we brainstorm, we accept all ideas. Tell students to write their lists in their books.

4. Call on a reporter to share their group's list of issues with the whole class. Call on reporters from other groups to add information not mentioned.

> **Consider the Ideas Answers, p. 100**
> Students' answers will vary. Possible answers:
> Pollution–resonsible for recycling; Health–responsible for eating well and exercising.

Prepare and Speak

Gather Ideas

A (5 minutes)

Direct students to read the statements. Tell students to check the statements they agree with. Have them work individually.

▶ *Listening and Speaking 3, page 101*

Tip for Critical Thinking (1 minute)

1. Read the tip aloud.

2. Point out that it is important to be able to support one's ideas and opinions. Explain that giving reasons helps people to better understand your position, and that it is easier to convince or persuade people to adopt a viewpoint if they can understand why they should do so.

Organize Ideas

B (10 minutes)

1. Tell students they are going to choose two statements from Activity A that they agreed with and one statement they disagreed with. Encourage them to choose the statements they felt most strongly about, either positively or negatively,

since this will make the activity more interesting.

2. Tell students to copy the statements in the correct places in the outline and write their reasons for their opinions in the space provided. Encourage them to use notes for their reasons since they should not read directly from their books.

Tip for Success (1 minute)

1. Read the tip aloud.

2. Point out that taking notes is useful to help you remember the main points when many people are participating in a discussion.

Critical Q: Expansion Activity

Identifying reasons

1. Tell students they are going to practice identifying reasons for someone's opinion.

2. Tell students that when they have their group discussion, they should listen for the reasons that the other group members give to support their opinions. Have students write each group member's opinion and the things he or she said to support it.

3. Ask students to check their understanding of their group members' reasons for their opinions at the end of the discussion. If they have not identified the reasons correctly, ask students to reflect on the language they heard which may have led to the misunderstanding.

Speak

C (10–15 minutes)

1. Review the checklist on page 102. Ask students to read the checklist. Elicit any questions.

2. Put students in groups to talk about their opinions about whether or not we are responsible for the world we live in. Remind them not to read directly from their outlines.

3. Ask students to choose a group leader. If students are reluctant to choose a leader, choose a student who is outgoing and capable of leading.

4. Have the leader open the discussion by asking the group members about one of the statements in Activity A. Remind students to limit their discussion to the issues in Activity A so that the discussion stays on track.

5. Use the unit assignment rubric on page 54 of this *Teacher's Handbook* to score each student's participation in the discussion.

6. Monitor students' performance as they work in pairs. Call on students you did not have a chance to monitor to present a summary of their discussion.

Alternative Unit Assignments

Assign or have students choose one of these assignments to do instead of, or in addition, to the unit assignment.

1. In some countries, companies employ children in poor conditions, working long hours for little money. What can be done to prevent this, and what action should be taken against such companies?

2. Imagine a teacher keeps a whole class after school because of the bad behavior of one or two students. What do you think of this idea of "collective responsibility," which punishes everyone for the mistakes of a few people? Form a group and discuss your ideas.

 For an additional unit assignment, have students visit *Q Online Practice*.

Check and Reflect

Check

A (5 minutes)

1. Direct students to read and complete the Self-Assessment checklist.

2. Ask for a show of hands for how many students gave all or mostly yes answers. Congratulate them on their success. Discuss the steps they can take if an item on the checklist was difficult for them.

 Reflect

B (5 minutes)

Refer students to the learning outcome on page 85. Tell them to talk with their partners about whether they achieved the learning outcome. Elicit the answers to the Unit Question that students came up with at the beginning of class.

▶ *Listening and Speaking 3, page 103*

Track Your Success

1. Have students circle the words and phrases they have learned in this unit. Suggest that students go back through the unit to review any words they have forgotten.

2. Have students check the skills they have mastered. If students need more practice to feel confident about their proficiency in a skill, point out the page numbers and encourage them to review.

3. Read the learning outcome aloud. Ask students if they feel that they have met the outcome.

Unit Assignment Rubric

Student name: _____

Date: _____

Unit Assignment: *Take part in a group discussion.*

20 = Presentation element was completely successful (at least 90% of the time).
15 = Presentation element was mostly successful (at least 70% of the time).
10 = Presentation element was partially successful (at least 50% of the time).
 0 = Presentation element was not successful.

Take part in a group discussion	20 points	15 points	10 points	0 points
Student easily explained opinions about whether we are responsible for the world we live in (without long pauses or reading) and was easy to understand (spoke clearly and at a good speed).				
Student used correct question tag forms.				
Student used appropriate question tag intonation.				
Student used vocabulary from the unit.				
Student was able to give reasons for his or her opinions.				

Total points: _____

Comments:

Unit QUESTION
How can advertisers change our behavior?

Advertising

LISTENING • identifying fact and opinion
VOCABULARY • context clues to identify meaning
GRAMMAR • modals expressing attitude
PRONUNCIATION • intonation in questions
SPEAKING • giving and supporting your opinions

LEARNING OUTCOME

State and support your opinions concerning the influence of advertising on our behavior.

▶ *Listening and Speaking 3, pages 104–105*
Preview the Unit

Learning Outcome

1. Ask for a volunteer to read the unit skills and then the unit learning outcome.

2. Explain: *The learning outcome is what you are expected to be able to do by the unit's end. You are going to be evaluated on how well you meet this outcome. With this in mind, you should focus on learning skills (Listening, Vocabulary, Grammar, Pronunciation, Speaking) that will support your goal of stating and supporting your opinions concerning the influence of advertising on our behavior. This can also help you act as mentors in the classroom to help the other students meet this outcome.*

A (10 minutes)

1. Prepare students for thinking about the topic by asking them where they see ads or commercials, for example, on TV, on the Internet, at movie theaters, on billboards, etc. Ask which ads or commercials they remember. Elicit why they remember these. Share your own recollections of memorable ads and commercials to spark discussion if necessary.

2. Put students in pairs or small groups to discuss the first four questions.

3. Call on volunteers to share their ideas with the class. Ask questions: *Why do you watch the commercials? Do you like any particular commercial? Why? If you don't watch them, what do you do during the commercial breaks? Why don't you watch the commercials? Do you recall any Internet ads that attracted your attention? Why did they attract your attention?*

4. Focus students' attention on the photo. Have a volunteer describe the photo to the class. Read the questions aloud.

Activity A Answers, p. 105
1. Students may get something to eat, channel surf, text or phone friends during the commercial breaks.
2. Students may or may not click on Internet ads, and they may or may not buy things. Students may purchase clothing, music, or electronics on the Internet.
3. The man is looking at the TV or the convertible sports car. Students may say he feels tired of walking and carrying packages and is interested in buying the car, or that he may wish that he could afford to buy the TV or the car.

B (15 minutes)

1. Introduce the Unit Question, "How can advertisers change our behavior?" Ask related information questions or questions about personal experience to help students prepare for answering the unit question, which is more abstract. *What is the goal of advertisers (*to make us buy*)? How can they make us do this? Why do they have famous athletes and actors endorsing products? Why do they have attractive people in advertisements? What other techniques do they use?*

2. Label four pieces of poster paper: Trust and Familiarity, New and Different, Rich and Famous, and Identify with a Group. Place them in the corners of the room.

3. Explain that each poster represents a feeling that advertising appeals to in order to influence consumers' behavior. Ask students to read and consider the unit question and then to stand in the corner next to the poster that best represents the feeling that they believe influences most consumers.

4. Direct the groups in each corner to talk amongst themselves about the reasons for their answers. Tell them to choose a recorder to write the answers on the poster paper.

5. Call on volunteers from each corner to share their opinions with the class.

6. Leave the posters up for students to refer to at the end of the unit.

Activity B Answers, p. 105
Possible answers: Advertisers can change our behavior by manipulating our emotions through the use of beautiful, successful people, or by appealing to a desire for prestige, to make us want to buy things; Advertisers can change our behavior by making their products look very attractive to us and showing us how they can make our lives better and easier; Advertisers can change our behavior by using actors and athletes to make their products look good.

The Q Classroom

CD2, Track 14

1. Play *The Q Classroom.* Use the example from the audio to help students continue the conversation. Ask: *According to the students, why does advertising work? Why is it important that you hear the name of a company over and over? According to Felix, why might someone buy something new, even if they don't need it?*

2. On the audio, students mention that advertising makes companies seem familiar and then consumers trust them, which results in consumers buying their goods and services. Elicit students' opinion on this issue. Ask students to support their opinions with examples.

▶ *Listening and Speaking 3, page 106*

C (10 minutes)

1. Tell students they are going to answer a questionnaire on types of advertising. Ask students to read the questionnaire. Elicit any questions about vocabulary.

2. Explain that students should check how often they notice these ads in their daily life. Tell students to think about the things they do and places they go on a typical day. Point out that they need not remember the company or product that is being advertised, just that they are aware of the presence of advertising.

Activity C Answers, p. 106
Students' answers will vary.

D (15 minutes)

1. Put students in pairs to compare their answers.

2. Draw a T-chart on the board. Write the headings "Advantages" and "Disadvantages" in the top of the T-chart. Make a separate row for each type of advertising. Tell the pairs to make their own T-chart and use it to take notes during their discussion.

3. Remind students to talk about which type of advertising they pay most attention to in their discussions.

4. Assign one type of advertising to each pair. Call a student to the board to write the advantages and disadvantages of that type of advertising.

5. Review the information as a class. Elicit which types of advertising students pay most attention to.

Activity D Answers, p. 106
Students' answers will vary. Possible answers: TV-advantages: you can reach a lot of people at once; disadvantages: it's easy for people to change the channel. I pay most attention to magazine ads.

MULTILEVEL OPTION

Group lower-level students and assist them with the task. Ask higher-level students to brainstorm other places where they notice advertising, for example, on buses, in the subway, or on people's clothing. Tell them to consider the advantages and disadvantages of these types of advertising.

LISTENING

▶ *Listening and Speaking 3, page 107*

LISTENING 1: Advertising Techniques

VOCABULARY (15 minutes)

1. Direct students to read the words in bold.

2. Model correct pronunciation of the words. Say each word and have students repeat.

3. Ask students to read the sentences and choose the correct answer.

4. Put students in pairs to check their answers.

5. Ask volunteers to read their answers. Elicit or provide corrections as necessary.

Group lower-level students and assist them with the task. Point out the cues in the sentences that will help them to choose the correct word. Give them additional sentences to help them practice the difficult vocabulary. For example: *Sometimes it's difficult for young people to **relate** to adults; I have an annoying advertising **jingle** stuck in my head. I can't stop humming it.*

Have higher-level students complete the activity individually and then compare answers with a partner. Tell the pairs to write an additional sample sentence for each word. Have volunteers write one of their sentences on the board. Correct the sentences with the whole class, focusing on the use of the vocabulary word rather than other grammatical issues.

Vocabulary Answers, p. 107
1. a; **2.** c; **3.** a; **4.** b; **5.** c;
6. b; **7.** b; **8.** c; **9.** b; **10.** a

 For additional practice with the vocabulary, have students visit *Q Online Practice*.

 Listening and Speaking 3, page 108

Tip for Success (1 minute)

Read the tip aloud. Point out that students may want to organize their notebooks according to unit or class, depending on how they remember information best.

PREVIEW LISTENING 1 (5 minutes)

1. Direct students to look at the photo. Ask: *What does the cowboy make you think of? Why? Have you ever seen cowboys used in advertising? What were the products? How did the image of the cowboy help sell the product?*

2. Read the introductory paragraph aloud. Brainstorm the possible products that might be mentioned on the radio. Encourage students to narrow their responses by asking them to think about the vocabulary. Ask: *Can you recall any of the techniques from the vocabulary being used on the radio? What goods or services did they promote?*

Preview Listening 1 Answers, p. 108
Answers will vary. In the listening, the goods and services mentioned are: home security, chocolate, a rodeo event, a restaurant, and deodorant.

Listening 1 Background Note

Advertising is a field that draws a lot of creative talent. People who are skilled at writing, music, fine arts, and visual arts are often drawn to careers in advertising. It is also known for innovation in film and video. Advertising is one of the few fields in which creative people can make a good living.

 Listening and Speaking 3, page 109

LISTEN FOR MAIN IDEAS (5 minutes)

CD2, Track 15

1. Ask students to read the ads and techniques. Elicit any questions or difficulties about them.

2. Play the audio and have students match the ads and techniques individually.

3. Elicit the answers from the class.

Main Idea Answers, p. 109
1. c; **2.** d; **3.** a; **4.** e; **5.** b

LISTEN FOR DETAILS (10 minutes)

CD2, Track 16

1. Direct students to read the sentences before they listen again. Elicit any questions about them.

2. As you play the audio, have students listen and write *T* or *F*.

3. Have students compare their answers with a partner.

4. Replay the audio so that the partners can check their answers.

5. Go over the answers with the class.

Listen for Details Answers, p. 109
1. T; **2.** F; **3.** T; **4.** F; **5.** F; **6.** F; **7.** T

 For additional practice with listening comprehension, have students visit *Q Online Practice*.

WHAT DO YOU THINK? (10 minutes)

1. Ask students to read the questions and reflect on their answers.

2. Seat students in small groups and assign roles: a group leader to make sure everyone contributes, a note-taker to record the group's ideas, a reporter to share the group's ideas with the class, and a timekeeper to watch the clock.

3. Give students five minutes to discuss the questions. Call time if conversations are winding down. Allow them an extra minute or two if necessary.

4. Call on each group's reporter to share ideas with the class.

> **What Do You Think? Answers, p. 109**
> Students' answers will vary. Possible answers:
> 1. Ben's diner because it is catchy.
> 2. Emotional appeal since it causes the strongest reaction.
> 3. Student can talk about radio ads they have heard in English or their own language.

Learning Outcome

Use the learning outcome to frame the purpose and relevance of Listening 1. Ask: *What did you learn from Listening 1 that prepares you to state your opinion about advertisers and their techniques? What did you learn that will help you explain how advertising influences your behavior?*

▶ *Listening and Speaking 3, page 110*

Listening Skill:
Identifying fact and opinion (5 minutes)

1. Ask students to read the information about the difference between a fact and an opinion. Elicit any difficulties or questions.

2. Check comprehension by drawing a T-chart on the board. Label the headings Fact and Opinion.

3. Elicit other facts and opinions. For example: *This language institute is located in (name of your location). This language institute is the best one in the area.*

4. As a class, brainstorm language that indicates a fact (dates, measurements, locations, prices, etc.). Repeat with language that indicates an opinion (adjectives such as *good, bad, better, worse, best, worst,* etc.)

A (5 minutes)
◗)) CD2, Track 17

1. Tell students they are going to listen to three sentences and they need to determine whether each is a fact or an opinion.

2. Play the audio while students circle *fact* or *opinion*. If necessary, pause or play the audio again.

3. Check the answers as a class. Elicit the words or information that led students to their answers.

> **Activity A Answers, p. 110**
> 1. fact; 2. opinion; 3. opinion

B (10 minutes)
◗)) CD2, Track 18

1. Tell students they are going to listen to statements from another ad describing a personal computer.

2. Play the audio while students circle their answers. Pause or play the audio again if necessary.

3. Call on volunteers to read their answers. Elicit the words or information that led students to their answers.

> **Activity B Answers, p. 110**
> 1. opinion; 2. fact;   3. fact;
> 4. opinion; 5. opinion; 6. fact

Tip for Success (1 minute)

Read the tip aloud. Point out that students may want to apply these techniques when listening to advertisements on the radio or television. Doing so will make them smarter consumers.

 For additional practice with identifying fact and opinion, have students visit *Q Online Practice.*

▶ *Listening and Speaking 3, page 111*

LISTENING 2:
Advertising Ethics and Standards

VOCABULARY (10 minutes)

1. Direct students to read the words and their definitions. Elicit any difficulties or questions.

2. Model correct pronunciation of the words. Say each word and have students repeat.

3. Ask students to complete the sentences.

4. Put students in pairs to check their answers.

5. Ask volunteers to read their answers.

> **Vocabulary Answers, p. 111**
> 1. refund;   2. mislead;   3. aimed at;
> 4. injury;   5. withdraw;   6. monitor;
> 7. competitor; 8. evidence;   9. deliberately;
> 10. regulations

MULTILEVEL OPTION

Group lower-level students and assist them with the task. Point out the cues in the words that will help them to choose the correct answer, for example the prefix *re-* in *refund* indicates again, so the word indicates *to fund again.*

---

1. We need **regulations** to make sure consumers are protected.
2. My sister fell at the shopping mall, but luckily, she didn't get a serious **injury**.

   Have higher-level students complete the activity individually and then compare answers with a partner. Tell the pairs to write an additional sentence for each word. Have volunteers write one of their sentences on the board. Correct the sentences with the whole class, focusing on the use of the vocabulary word rather than other grammatical issues.

 For additional practice with the vocabulary, have students visit *Q Online Practice.*

▶ *Listening and Speaking 3, page 112*

PREVIEW LISTENING 2 (5 minutes)

Read the paragraph aloud. Explain that the FTC is responsible for regulating trade, or buying and selling, in the United States.

Listening 2 Background Note

The Federal Trade Commission (FTC) is an independent agency of the U.S. government. It was established by President Woodrow Wilson in 1915. It is responsible for keeping American business competition free and fair and was established as part of a program to check the growth of monopoly and preserve competition as an effective regulator of business. The FTC has five members, and no more than three of them may be members of the same political party.

LISTEN FOR MAIN IDEAS (5 minutes)

CD2, Track 19

1. Ask students to read the statements. Elicit any difficulties with vocabulary or concepts.
2. Play the audio and have students complete the activity individually.
3. Call on volunteers to share their answers.

   Listen for Main Idea Answers, p. 112
   1. T; **2.** F; **3.** F; **4.** T; **5.** F; **6.** T; **7.** T; **8.** F

LISTEN FOR DETAILS (5 minutes)

CD2, Track 20

1. Tell students they are going to listen again. Ask them to read the sentences and answer choices. Elicit any questions or difficulties.

2. Play the audio while students choose the best answer to complete each sentence.
3. Have students compare answers with a partner.
4. Go over the answers with the class.

   Listen for Details Answers, p. 112
   1. b; **2.** a; **3.** b; **4.** c; **5.** a; **6.** a; **7.** a; **8.** a

 For additional practice with listening comprehension, have students visit *Q Online Practice.*

▶ *Listening and Speaking 3, page 114*

WHAT DO YOU THINK?

A (10 minutes)

1. Ask students to read the questions and reflect on their answers.
2. Seat students in small groups and assign roles: a group leader to make sure everyone contributes, a note-taker to record the group's ideas, a reporter to share the group's ideas with the class, and a timekeeper to watch the clock.
3. Give students five minutes to discuss the questions. Call time if conversations are winding down. Allow them an extra minute or two if necessary.
4. Call on each group's reporter to share ideas with the class.

   Activity A Answers, p. 114
   Students' answers will vary. Possible answers:
   1. Yes, because you see the product but are not bothered by an annoying ad; No, because it's too subtle. Many movies and TV shows use product placement ads.
   2. Student may say children or teenagers because they are younger and more easily influenced.

B (10 minutes]

1. Have students continue working their small groups to discuss the questions in Activity B. Tell them to choose a new leader, recorder, reporter, and timekeeper.
2. For question 1, encourage students to reflect on the discussion from the *Q classroom*, as well as Listenings 1 and 2.
3. Call on the new reporter to share the group's answers to the questions.

Answers will vary. Possible answers:
1. It's cheap, healthy, beautiful, modern, prestigious.
2. cheap–appliances, books, household items;
   healthy–food, vitamins, skin care;
   beautiful–makeup, hair products, clothing;
   modern–electronics, cars;
   prestigious–electronics, cars, clothing.

Tip for Critical Thinking (1 minute)

Read the tip aloud. Point out that we need to evaluate in our academic as well as our everyday lives. Practicing this skill is important to academic success as well as to success as a consumer in the marketplace.

Critical Q: Expansion Activity

Evaluating Advertising Slogans

1. Put students in small groups of three or four. Review the meaning of the word *slogan*.
2. Give the groups five minutes to design one advertising slogan for a product of their choice. Tell them to choose a target group for the product and to make the slogan as persuasive as possible for this group.
3. Have each group present its slogan. Elicit from the class the target audience for the slogan as well as how effective the slogan is and why.

Learning Outcome

Use the learning outcome to frame the purpose and relevance of Listenings 1 and 2 and the Critical Q activity of evaluating an advertising slogan. Ask: *What did you learn from the listenings and evaluating advertising slogans that prepares you to state and support your opinions about advertising's influence on our behavior?*

Vocabulary Skill: Context clues to identify meaning (10 minutes)

1. Direct students to read the information in the first paragraph silently.
2. Check comprehension: *What does* context *mean? How can it help us to understand a word's meaning?*
3. Ask students to read the remaining information. Elicit a way based on part of speech that students can determine that *circulation* is a noun (*It is preceded by* a, *which is used before nouns*).
4. Elicit any questions or difficulties about the information.

Skill Note

Point out that being able to determine a word's meaning from context is an important skill because there may be times when a dictionary is unavailable. Similarly, in testing situations, dictionaries may not be permitted.

▶ *Listening and Speaking 3, page 115*

A (10 minutes)

1. Review the first sentence with the class. Ask students to work individually to underline the context clues in each sentence. Point out that there may be one or two context clues for each.
2. Put students in pairs to review their answers. Go over the answers with the class.

Activity A Answers, p. 115
2. same ads all day / over and over;
3. the most expensive;
4. sell more;
5. ads / everywhere;
6. couldn't stop humming for days.

MULTILEVEL OPTION

Group lower-level students and assist them with the task. Point out the cues in the sentences that will help them to choose the correct answer, for example in sentence 2, *same* and *over and over* have related meanings.

Have higher-level students work in small groups to choose five vocabulary words from the two vocabulary sections to write sentences in which the word's meaning can be guessed from context. Ask the groups to present their sentences for the class and elicit the context clues that enable them to guess the words.

B (5 minutes)

1. Keep students in pairs, but have students do the activity individually.
2. Have students compare their answers with their partner. Call on volunteers to read their answers.

Activity B Answers, p. 115
1. push;   2. eye-catching;   3. prime time;
4. hype;   5. catchy;   6. tedious

web For additional practice with using context clues to identify meaning, have students visit *Q Online Practice*.

▶ *Listening and Speaking 3, page 116*

SPEAKING

Grammar:
Modals expressing attitude (10 minutes)

1. Read the information about modal verbs aloud.

2. Check comprehension by asking questions: *What kind of verbs are modal verbs? What four kinds of attitude can they express? What is an example of a modal verb that expresses prohibition? Is must / must not more common in conversation than in writing?*

Skill Note

Write the subject pronouns, *I, you, he, she, it, we,* and *they* on the board. Point out that with modal verbs, the form is the same for each of these subjects.

A (10 minutes)
CD2, Track 21

1. Tell students they are going to circle the modal verbs they hear. Ask them to read the conversation. Elicit any questions or difficulties.

2. Play the audio while students circle their answers.

3. Put students in pairs to check their answers. Check the answers as a class.

4. Have students practice the conversation.

> **Activity A Answers, p. 116**
> **1.** don't have to; **2.** don't have to; **3.** can't;
> **4.** should; **5.** shouldn't

▶ *Listening and Speaking 3, page 117*

B (10 minutes)

1. Put the pairs into groups to discuss the questions.

2. Assign a note-taker and a reporter for each group.

3. Call on the reporter for each group to present the group's opinions for each question.

> **Activity B Answers, p. 117**
> Student's answers will vary. Possible answers:
> **1.** Ads that make people angry should still be allowed; advertisers don't have to make people happy.
> **2.** Ads that mislead people must not be allowed. They have to tell the truth.

 For additional practice with *modals*, have students visit *Q Online Practice.*

Pronunciation *Part 1:*
Intonation in questions (10 minutes)

CD2, Track 22

1. Read the information about intonation in questions.

2. Check comprehension by asking: *Is intonation the same for all questions? What is the intonation at the end of yes/no questions? What is the intonation at the end of wh- questions?*

3. Tell students to read the questions from the interview while they listen to the audio. Have them run their fingers along the arrows as they listen to the audio.

4. Play the audio again as a model for the students. Stop for students to repeat the sentences with correct intonation.

A (10 minutes)
CD2, Track 23

1. Have students read the sentences.

2. Tell students to circle whether the sentence has rising or falling intonation. Encourage them to write an arrow above the sentence, as in the examples in the preceding section, to show the intonation as they listen.

3. Play the audio while students write their arrows and circle their answers.

4. Elicit the answers from volunteers. If there are any disagreements, play the audio again to confirm.

> **Activity A Answers, p. 117**
> **1.** rise; **2.** fall; **3.** rise; **4.** rise; **5.** fall

B (5 minutes)
CD2, Track 24

1. Tell students to repeat the questions, using the same intonation that they hear.

2. Play the audio, pausing as necessary for students to repeat.

▶ *Listening and Speaking 3, page 118*

Pronunciation *Part 2:*
Intonation in questions (10 minutes)

CD2, Track 25

1. Read the information about intonation in statements as questions.

2. Check comprehension by asking: *Is intonation the same for statements used as a question as it is for traditional questions? What is the intonation for a statement? What is the intonation for a statement used as a question?*

3. Tell students to read the sentences while they listen to the audio. Have them run their fingers along the arrows as they listen to the audio.

4. Play the audio again as a model for the students. Stop for students to repeat the sentences with correct intonation.

C (5 minutes)
CD2, Track 26

1. Tell students they are going to listen to some sentences that are spoken as either statements or questions.

2. Do the example with the students. Remind them to put the punctuation at the end of the sentence.

3. Have students complete the activity. Check as a class. Replay the audio as necessary to clarify answers.

> **Activity C Answers, p. 118**
> **1.** question; **2.** statement; **3.** question;
> **4.** statement; **5.** question; **6.** question;
> **7.** statement

D (5 minutes)
CD2, Track 27

1. Put students in pairs.

2. Play the audio again for students, pausing after each sentence for students to repeat.

3. Tell students to take turns saying the sentences from Activity C in a random order and using the intonation (question or statement) of their choice.

4. Call on several students to say a sentence for the class. Ask the class to determine if the intonation was for a question or statement.

 For additional practice with question and statement intonation, have students visit *Q Online Practice*.

▶ *Listening and Speaking 3, page 119*
Speaking Skill: Giving and supporting your opinions (5 minutes)

1. Direct students to read the information about giving and supporting opinions.

2. Point out that an opinion that is presented clearly and is supported is usually more persuasive than one that is not.

3. Check comprehension: *What are some of the phrases used for giving opinions? What are some phrases used for supporting an opinion?*

21ST CENTURY SKILLS

Being able to see another side of one's opinion is an important skill for success in the workplace and university. It can be difficult to do this because it requires us to evaluate our opinions critically. Help students to begin to develop this important skill through practice. Conduct "short speech" activities throughout whichever unit you are working on. (This will usually help them prepare for the unit assignment as well.) Assign a very specific topic for which students can have an opinion, for example, in this unit, "Everyone can be influenced by advertising." Tell students to prepare a 30-second speech advocating the viewpoint counter to theirs. Pass out small note cards for students to plan a 30-second speech advocating the opposite opinion. Then put the students in groups and have them deliver their short speech to the group.

A (10 minutes)
CD2, Track 28

1. Tell students they are going to listen to a conversation about an ad. Have students read the conversation. Elicit any questions or difficulties.

2. Play the audio while students complete the conversation. Pause as necessary to give students time to write.

3. Put students in pairs to compare their answers. Call on volunteers to share their answers.

4. Play the audio again to clarify any difficulties.

5. Give pairs time to practice the conversations.

6. Call on volunteers to perform for the class.

> **Activity A Answers, p. 119**
> **1.** If you ask me; **2.** because;
> **3.** As far as I'm concerned; **4.** For instance;
> **5.** In my opinion

▶ *Listening and Speaking 3, page 120*
B (10 minutes)

1. Keep students in pairs. Tell them to discuss the effectiveness of ads that feature famous people.

2. Remind them to use the phrases for giving and supporting opinions. Elicit some of the things they should do when discussing with a partner, for example, maintain eye contact, give reasons, take turns, etc.

3. Monitor students' conversations for their use of phrases as well as their intonation.

 For additional practice with giving and supporting opinions, have students visit *Q Online Practice*.

Expansion Activity: Opinions about advertisements (10 minutes)

1. Put students into pairs.

2. Ask them to think about three different kinds of advertisements they have seen recently.

3. Have them tell their partners about the three different advertisements they saw, and the advantages and disadvantages of each type. Remind them to support their opinions with reasons and examples, and to use the phrases from the Speaking Skill box on page 119 of the student book.

4. Elicit answers from volunteers.

Q Unit Assignment:
Take part in a group discussion

Unit Question (5 minutes)

Refer students to the ideas they discussed at the beginning of the unit about how advertisers try to change our behavior. Cue students if necessary by asking specific questions about the content of the unit: *What are some of the techniques that advertisers use to influence consumers? What are the different types of products that may be marketed with these various techniques?*

Learning Outcome

1. Tie the unit assignment to the unit learning outcome. Say: *The outcome for this unit is to discuss how advertisers can influence our behavior. This unit assignment is going to let you show your skill in participating in a discussion. Participating in a group discussion is a useful skill because it allows people to share their experiences, viewpoints, and opinion. In doing so, we have the opportunity to educate and learn from others.*

2. Explain that you are going to use a rubric similar to their Self-Assessment checklist on page 122 to grade their unit assignment.

Consider the Ideas (10 minutes)

1. Tell students they are going to choose one of the topics and discuss their ideas with a partner. Ask students to quickly read the three topics and their questions. Elicit any difficulties or questions.

2. Remind students to keep the Unit Question in mind as they discuss. Also remind them to focus on their intonation in questions and statements.

3. Put students in pairs to choose their topics and discuss them. Tell them to take notes during their discussion.

4. Call on volunteers to share their opinions and give their reasons.

▶ *Listening and Speaking 3, page 121*

Prepare and Speak

Gather Ideas

A (5 minutes)

1. Direct students to write notes on what they can recall from their discussion of the Consider the Ideas activity. Encourage them to add any new ideas they have thought of.

2. Point out that students should write as much as they can remember since they will have the opportunity to select the most important information in the next activity.

3. Remind students not to write complete sentences. If necessary, elicit the main points of writing notes (main ideas, no complete sentences, etc.).

4. Tell students to compare their notes with their partner's.

Organize Ideas

B (10 minutes)

1. Tell students to choose the most important ideas from their notes in Activity A and complete the outline.

2. Remind students not to write complete sentences, just the most important points they need to mention.

▶ *Listening and Speaking 3, page 122*

Speak

C (10–15 minutes)

1. Review the checklist on page 122. Ask students to read it. Elicit any questions.

2. Put students in groups according to which topic they chose. Remind them not to read directly from their outlines.

3. Ask students to choose a group leader. If students are reluctant to choose a leader, choose a student who is outgoing and capable of leading. Remind students of the role of the group leader (to ensure everyone speaks, to keep the discussion going, etc).

4. Have the leader open the discussion by asking the group members about their opinions on the topic. Remind students to limit their discussion to the issues outlined in Activity B so that the discussion stays on track.

5. Use the Unit Assignment Rubric on page 65 of this *Teacher's Handbook* to score each student's participation in the discussion.

6. Monitor students' performance as they work in groups. Call on students you did not have a chance to monitor to present a summary of their discussion.

Alternative Unit Assignments

Assign or have students choose one of these assignments to do instead of, or in addition, to the unit assignment.

1. Think of an ad you know, or find one online, on TV, or in a magazine or newspaper. Using the chart below as a guide, make notes and prepare to talk about the ad.

Type of ad (radio, TV, etc.):	
Name of product it is advertising:	
Target audience:	
What you like about the ad:	
What you don't like about the ad:	
Techniques it uses:	
How it could be improved:	

Form a group and present your analysis of the ad you chose. Remember to explain your reasons clearly and give examples wherever possible. After you finish, be prepared to answer any questions your classmates may have.

2. Make your own radio ad. In a group, discuss your ideas and then plan your ad. Use the worksheet from question 1 to help you.

Check and Reflect

Check

A (5 minutes)

1. Direct students to read and complete the Self-Assessment checklist.

2. Ask for a show of hands for how many students gave all or mostly yes answers.

3. Congratulate them on their success. Discuss the steps they can take if an item on the checklist was difficult for them. For example, if they had trouble with intonation, they can record themselves speaking and ask another student to listen to them.

Reflect

B (5 minutes)

Refer students to the learning outcome on page 105. Tell them to talk with their partners about whether they achieved the learning outcome. Elicit the answers to the Unit Question that students came up with at the beginning of class. Encourage them to flip through the unit as they discuss the new things they learned and new answers they may have to the Unit Question.

▶ *Listening and Speaking 3, page 123*

Track Your Success

1. Have students circle the words they have learned in this unit. Suggest that students go back through the unit to review any words they have forgotten.

2. Have students check the skills they have mastered. If students need more practice to feel confident about their proficiency in a skill, point out the page numbers and encourage them to review.

3. Read the learning outcome aloud. Ask students if they feel that they have met the outcome.

Unit 6   Advertising

Unit Assignment Rubric

Student name: _____

Date: _____

Unit Assignment: *Take part in a group discussion.*

20 = Presentation element was completely successful (at least 90% of the time).
15 = Presentation element was mostly successful (at least 70% of the time).
10 = Presentation element was partially successful (at least 50% of the time).
 0 = Presentation element was not successful.

Take part in a group discussion	20 points	15 points	10 points	0 points
Student spoke easily (without long pauses or reading) about the influence of advertising on our behavior and was easy to understand (spoke clearly and at a good speed).				
Student expressed attitude using correct modal verb forms.				
Student used appropriate statement and question intonation.				
Student used vocabulary from the unit.				
Student was able to give and support their opinion.				

Total points: _____

Comments:

Unit QUESTION
What risks are good to take?

Risk

LISTENING • identifying amounts; cardinal and ordinal numbers
VOCABULARY • word families
GRAMMAR • past perfect
PRONUNCIATION • contraction of *had*
SPEAKING • giving a short presentation

LEARNING OUTCOME

Give a short presentation on a risk you have taken, explaining your reasons for taking that risk.

▶ *Listening and Speaking 3, pages 124–125*
Preview the Unit

Learning Outcome

1. Ask for a volunteer to read the unit skills and then the unit learning outcome.

2. Explain: *The learning outcome is what you are expected to be able to do by the unit's end. You are going to be evaluated on how well you meet this outcome. With this in mind, you should focus on learning skills (Listening, Vocabulary, Grammar, Pronunciation, Speaking) that will support your goal of giving a short presentation on a risk you have taken, explaining your reasons for taking that risk. This can also help you act as mentors in the classroom to help the other students meet this outcome.*

A (10 minutes)

1. Prepare students for thinking about the topic by asking students what they think constitutes a risk. Elicit the characteristics of an activity that make it a risk. Start the discussion by asking questions such as: *Does a risk have to involve physical danger? Must it involve the possibility of losing something, for example money?* Generate a class definition of *risk* and write it on the board.

2. Put students in pairs or small groups to discuss the first five questions.

3. Call on volunteers to share their ideas with the class. Ask questions to facilitate the discussion: *Are some activities more risky than others? Why? What makes a risk worth taking? How do people decide that a risk is worth taking?*

4. Focus students' attention on the photo. Have a volunteer describe the photo to the class. Read the questions aloud.

Activity A Answers, p. 125
Possible answers:
1. Risks people take can include physical, financial, or emotional risks. Examples of physical risk include sports and expeditions. Examples of financial risk include some investments and perhaps education. Examples of emotional risks include confronting someone.
2. Students will have different opinions about where to draw the line on taking risks.
3. The photo is a rocket launch. Student may say that this is a risk because it is very dangerous.

B (15 minutes)

1. Introduce the Unit Question, "What risks are good to take?" Ask related information questions or questions about personal experience to help students prepare for answering the Unit Question, which is more abstract. *What is the reward of taking a risk? How do people evaluate the risk of an activity in relation to its reward? Are some rewards worth more than others?*

2. Read the unit question aloud. Point out that answers to the question can fall into the following categories: 1. Risks that offer personal financial benefits; 2. Risks that offer financial benefits to society or humanity; 3. Risks that offer personal benefits not related to finances; and 4. Risks that offer societal benefits not related to finances.

3. Give students a minute to silently consider their answers to the unit question.

4. Write each category at the top of four sheets of poster paper. Elicit answers for the question and make notes of the answers under the correct heading. Post the lists to refer to later in the unit.

Activity B Answers, p. 125
Possible answers: Risks that are worth taking are those for which the potential benefits of success outweigh the potential losses if the risk fails; The risks that are good to take have a greater benefit if successful than loss if unsuccessful; Good risks will give a very good reward if they are successful. They will not be very harmful if they fail.

The Q Classroom

CD2, Track 29

1. Play *The Q Classroom*. Use the example from the audio to help students continue the conversation. Ask: *What types of risks do the students mention* (social and professional)*? Why is it good to take social risks? What are the risks of changing jobs?*
2. On the audio, students mention that it is important to be careful about taking risks. Elicit students' opinions as to how one can be careful about taking risks. If necessary, begin the discussion by offering suggestions, for example, thinking about the effects on their family, their financial situation, etc.

Listening and Speaking 3, page 126

C (10 minutes)

1. Tell students they are going to answer a questionnaire to find out whether they are risk takers. Ask students to read the questionnaire. Elicit any questions about vocabulary.
2. Explain that students should check whether they have done the action, have never done the action but might do it, or have never done the action and they won't do it.
3. Have students complete the questionnaire and rate their answers according to the key at the bottom of the page.

Activity C Answers, p 126
Students' answers will vary.

D (10 minutes)

1. Put students in groups to compare their answers.
2. Tell students to review their answers and their results. Students should discuss whether they agree with the descriptions and give reasons and examples for their opinions.
3. Ask students to rank the members of their group from most willing to take risks to least willing to take risks.
4. Call on volunteers to report their group's findings.

MULTILEVEL OPTION

Group lower-level students and assist them with the task. Ask higher-level students to categorize the activities in the questionnaire into the following groups: physical risk taking, financial risk taking, and social risk taking. Tell them to categorize their answers to determine exactly what kind of risk taker they are, i.e., a physical, social, or financial risk taker.

Expansion Activity: Risks in real life (10 minutes)

1. Keep students in their groups from Activity D.
2. Ask students to think of risks they have taken in their lives. They should think about why it was a risk, why they took it, and if it was a good risk to take.
3. Have students share their risks with their groups.
4. Elicit answers from the groups.

LISTENING

Listening and Speaking 3, page 127

LISTENING 1: Financing a Dream

VOCABULARY (15 minutes)

1. Direct students to read the words and their definitions. Elicit any difficulties or questions.
2. Model correct pronunciation of the words. Say each word and have students repeat.
3. Ask students to complete the paragraph.
4. Put students in pairs to check their answers.
5. Ask volunteers to read their answers. Elicit or provide corrections as necessary.

MULTILEVEL OPTION

Group lower-level students and assist them with the task. Point out the cues in the sentences that will help them to choose the correct word. Give them additional sentences to help them practice the difficult vocabulary. For example: *I always prefer to pay cash instead of buying things with* ***credit****. A journalist's job is to* ***expose*** *the truth, even if this is dangerous or unpopular.*

Have higher-level students complete the activity individually and then compare answers with a partner. Tell the pairs to write an additional sample sentence for each word. Have volunteers write one of their sentences on the board. Correct the sentences with the whole class, focusing on the use of the vocabulary word rather than other grammatical issues.

Vocabulary Answers, p. 127
1. financial; **2.** income; **3.** credit; **4.** debt;
5. funds; **6.** embarrass; **7.** expose; **8.** model;
9. audience; **10.** threaten

 For additional practice with the vocabulary, have students visit *Q Online Practice*.

▶ *Listening and Speaking 3, page 128*

PREVIEW LISTENING 1 (5 minutes)

Read the introductory paragraph aloud. Ask students to think of two financial risks a filmmaker might take in order to make a movie. Tell students they should review their answers after the listening.

Preview Listening 1 Answers, p. 128
Possible answers: Filmmakers might lose all their savings or their homes.

Listening 1 Background Note

All the filmmakers mentioned in the listening are noted independent filmmakers. Independent films differ from mainstream, commercial movies in that they are created without the financial backing of a Hollywood studio. As a result, independent films typically have lower budgets and frequently, they are not marketed widely. They often rely on critical acclaim or word-of-mouth recommendations to attract their audiences.

LISTEN FOR MAIN IDEAS (5 minutes)

 CD2, Track 30

1. Explain that students are going to listen to the film critic's talk and check the risks that the filmmakers took when making their movies.

2. Ask students to read the information. Elicit any questions or difficulties.

3. Play the audio and have students check the risks individually.

4. Elicit the answers from the class.

Main Idea Answers, p. 128
Check items 1, 3, and 6.

▶ *Listening and Speaking 3, page 129*

LISTEN FOR DETAILS (10 minutes)

 CD2, Track 31

1. Direct students to read the names and types of financing before they listen again. Elicit any questions.

2. As you play the audio, have students listen and match the names with the types of financing.

3. Have students compare their answers with a partner.

4. Replay the audio so that the partners can check their answers. Go over the answers with the class.

Listen for Details Answers, p. 129
1. d; **2.** c; **3.** b; **4.** a; **5.** e

 For additional practice with listening comprehension, have students visit *Q Online Practice*.

WHAT DO YOU THINK? (10 minutes)

1. Ask students to read the questions and reflect on their answers.

2. Seat students in small groups and assign roles: a group leader to make sure everyone contributes, a note-taker to record the group's ideas, a reporter to share the group's ideas with the class, and a timekeeper to watch the clock.

3. Give students five minutes to discuss the questions. Call time if conversations are winding down. Allow them an extra minute or two if necessary.

4. Call on each group's reporter to share ideas with the class.

What Do You Think? Answers, p. 129
Answers will vary. Possible answers:
1. They wanted to make these films but did not have the money to do it.
2. My dream of getting a degree and a good job requires a financial risk since I'm spending a lot of money to make it happen.
3. Policemen or firefighters have jobs that have a lot of physical risk because they are often in life-threatening situations.

Learning Outcome

Use the learning outcome to frame the purpose and relevance of Listening 1. Ask: *What did you learn from Listening 1 that prepares you to give a short presentation on a risk you have taken? What did you learn that will help you explain your reasons for taking that risk?*

▶ *Listening and Speaking 3, page 130*

Listening Skill *Part 1*: Identifying amounts (15 minutes)

🔊 CD2, Tracks 32–34

1. Ask students to read the information about identifying amounts. Elicit any difficulties or questions.

2. Check comprehension by asking questions: *Do you write currency amounts in the same way that you hear them?*

3. Tell students to follow along in their books while they listen to the examples of currency amounts. Play track 32.

4. Review the currency symbols for dollars ($), pounds (£), and euros (€). Ask students to pay attention to the amount they hear.

5. Play track 33 and elicit how the amounts in the excerpt were spoken.

6. Tell students they are going to listen to another example of amounts, but this time they will hear the amounts as adjectives.

7. Play track 34 while students follow in their books. Pause for students to repeat the amounts in bold.

8. Tell students to read the information on amounts as adjectives. Ask: *Do we use a plural form in the adjective? (No)*

A (5 minutes)
🔊 CD2, Track 35

1. Read the directions aloud. Tell students to write the amounts as words, including hyphens if necessary. Point out that they don't need to write the dollar sign if the amount refers to money, because they will have written the word *dollar*.

2. Play the audio while students complete the sentences. If necessary, pause or replay the audio.

3. Check the answers as a class.

Activity A Answers, p. 130
1. one hundred and eighty thousand dollars;
2. ten dollars;
3. five-pound, three dollars;
4. four-hundred-seat;
5. five-hundred-dollar;
6. ten-question;
7. sixty pounds;
8. fifty-dollar

▶ *Listening and Speaking 3, page 131*

B (10 minutes)

1. Put students in pairs to ask and answer questions about the sentences in Activity A.

2. Call on volunteers to ask their questions. Elicit the answers from the class.

Activity B Answers, p. 131
Answers will vary. Possible answers:
2. How much are the cheapest tickets?
3. How much is the five-pound bag of sugar?
4. How many seats were in the theater?
5. What does that store sell?
6. What kind of survey did you take online?
7. How much does your suitcase weight?
8. What did Maria find on the sidewalk?

 For additional practice with amounts, have students visit *Q Online Practice*.

Listening Skill *Part 2*: Cardinal and ordinal numbers (5 minutes)

🔊 CD2, Track 36

1. Ask students to read the information about identifying cardinal and ordinal numbers. Elicit any difficulties or questions.

2. Check comprehension by asking questions: *What do most ordinal numbers end in? What kind of number is one? (cardinal) What kind of number is third? (ordinal).*

3. Tell students they are going to listen to some cardinal and ordinal numbers. Have them follow along in their books while they listen.

4. Play the audio, pausing for students to say the pairs of numbers.

C (10 minutes)
🔊 CD2, Track 37

1. Tell students to look at the first pair of sentences. Elicit the difference between them (The first has a cardinal number and the second has an ordinal number).

2. Tell students they are going to hear only one of the sentences from the pair. Have them check the sentence they hear.

3. Play the audio while students check the correct sentences.

4. Check as a class. Play the audio again to confirm.

> **Activity C Answers, p. 131**
> **1.** The seventh test can be taken this week.
> **2.** The nine students left an hour ago.
> **3.** I ate fifteen cookies.
> **4.** Did you receive the sixth email I sent you?
> **5.** Push the fourth button.

 Listening and Speaking 3, page 132

D (10 minutes)

CD2, Track 38

1. Play the audio again, pausing for students to repeat the sentences.

2. Put students in pairs. Tell them to choose a sentence from each pair to say to their partner.

3. Explain that their partner should hold up one finger if they hear the first sentence, or two if they hear the second. Tell them to change roles after one sentence from each pair has been read.

4. Monitor students' activity. Pay attention to the ending sound on the ordinal numbers.

 For additional practice with cardinal and ordinal numbers, have students visit *Q Online Practice*.

LISTENING 2: The Truth about the Loch Ness Monster

VOCABULARY (10 minutes)

1. Ask students to locate the bold words in each sentence. Model correct pronunciation and have students repeat the words.

2. Tell students to read the sentences and then write the word next to its definition below.

3. Put students in pairs to check their answers.

4. Ask volunteers to read their answers. Elicit or provide corrections as necessary.

> **Vocabulary Answers, p. 132**
> **a.** locate; **b.** solve; **c.** previous; **d.** investigate;
> **e.** invent; **f.** retire; **g.** reputation; **h.** prove;
> **i.** mystery; **j.** discover

 For additional practice with the vocabulary, have students visit *Q Online Practice*.

 Listening and Speaking 3, page 133

PREVIEW LISTENING 2 (5 minutes)

1. Read the paragraph aloud. Ask students to look at the photo of the Loch Ness Monster. Ask: *Do you believe it is real? Why or why not?*

2. Tell students to check the risks they think scientists might take. Tell them to review their answers after the listening.

Listening 2 Background Note

The Loch Ness Monster is believed by some to be a dinosaur-like creature that lives in Loch Ness, a lake in the Scottish highlands. The first reported sighting was in 1933, although evidence for its existence is based on controversial photographs and much-disputed sonar readings, and has never been scientifically proven.

LISTEN FOR MAIN IDEAS (5 minutes)

CD2, Track 39

1. Ask students to read the statements. Elicit any difficulties with vocabulary or concepts.

2. Play the audio and have students work individually to write *T* or *F*.

3. Call on volunteers to share their answers.

> **Listen for Main Idea Answers, p. 133**
> **1.** T; **2.** F; **3.** T; **4.** F; **5.** F; **6.** T

 Listening and Speaking 3, page 134

LISTEN FOR DETAILS (5 minutes)

CD2, Track 40

1. Tell students they are going to listen again. Ask them to read the questions and answer choices. Elicit any questions or difficulties.

2. Play the audio while students choose the correct answer.

3. Have students compare answers with a partner.

4. Go over the answers with the class.

> **Listen for Details Answers, p. 134**
> **1.** a, **2.** a, **3.** c, **4.** b, **5.** a, **6.** b, **7.** b

 For additional practice with listening comprehension, have students visit *Q Online Practice*.

❓ WHAT DO YOU THINK?

A (10 minutes)

1. Ask students to read the questions and reflect on their answers.

2. Seat students in small groups and assign roles: a group leader to make sure everyone contributes, a note-taker to record the group's ideas, a reporter to share the group's ideas with the class, and a timekeeper to watch the clock.

3. Give students five minutes to discuss the questions. Call time if conversations are winding down. Allow them an extra minute or two if necessary.

4. Call on each group's reporter to share ideas with the class.

> **Activity A Answers, p. 135**
> Students' answers will vary. Possible answers:
> **1.** He is willing to risk so much because he really believes in Nessie. He is different from most people in that he will risk his career and reputation for something that may not be true.
> **2.** People find mysteries interesting because they are unusual and cannot always be explained.

B (10 minutes)

1. Have students continue working in their small groups to discuss the questions in activity B. Tell them to choose a new leader, recorder, reporter, and timekeeper.

2. Recap the people talked about in the listening as well as the risks they took.

3. Call on the new reporter to share the group's answers to the questions.

> **Activity B Answers, p. 135**
> Answers will vary. Possible answers:
> **1.** Reputation: People, especially those with a lot of money, may not care what people think. Money: Some people value their reputation more than money because once lost, it may not be regained, but money, once lost, can be earned again.
> **2.** Student answers will vary depending on their willingness to take risks or their interests in those fields.

Vocabulary Skill: Word families
(10 minutes)

1. Direct students to read the information in the first paragraph and the definitions silently.

2. Check comprehension: *What is a word family? What is the root word for* invention *and* inventive? *What do these words mean?*

3. Ask students to read the remaining information. Elicit how understanding word families can increase vocabulary (*It is possible to add new words to it based on understanding a root word*).

4. Elicit any questions or difficulties about the information.

Tip for Critical Thinking (1 minute)

Read the tip aloud. Point out that categorizing is an extremely useful skill and that groups can be based on a various things, for example, meaning or theme, or even parts of speech.

Critical Q: Expansion Activity

Categorizing Techniques

1. Put students in small groups of three or four. Give each group a theme, e.g., inventions, explorations, investments, or education.

2. Assign a note-taker for each group and a reporter.

3. Tell the groups that they have five minutes to list as many words as they can that are related to the theme of their category. Encourage them to be creative as well as prepared to justify why each word is connected to the theme.

4. Call on the reporters to share the group's words with the class.

Learning Outcome

Use the learning outcome to frame the purpose and relevance of Listenings 1 and 2 and the Critical Q activity of categorizing. Ask: *What did you learn from the listenings that prepares you to identify a risk you have taken? What did you learn that will help you give a short presentation explaining your reasons for taking it?*

A (10 minutes)

1. Copy the first row of the chart on the board. Review the meaning and part of speech of each word in the first row.

2. Point out the suffixes that are attached to each word to create the different parts of speech (-*or* for noun, -*ive* for adjective, -*ly* on an adjective to create an adverb).

3. Put students in pairs to complete the chart. Point out that the shaded areas indicate no word is possible. Encourage them to use their dictionaries.

4. Go over the answers with the class.

Activity A Answers, p. 136
2. create, creator/creativity/creation, creative, creatively;
3. discover, discovery/discoverer;
4. embarrass, embarrassment, embarrassing, embarrassingly;
5. finance, finance(s), financial, financially;
6. locate, location;
7. prove, proof, proven;
8. solve, solution

MULTILEVEL OPTION

Group lower-level students and assist them with the task. Help them to remember other suffixes associated with different parts of speech, e.g., *-er* to turn verbs into nouns.

Have higher-level students work in small groups to choose one row and write a sentence for word. Review them as a class, focusing on whether the part of speech is used correctly.

B (5 minutes)

1. Keep students in pairs, but have students do the activity individually. Remind them they may have to change the form.

2. Have students compare their answers with their partner. Call on volunteers to read their answers.

Activity B Answers, p. 136
1. creative/inventive; **2.** solve; **3.** create;
4. finance; **5.** solution; **6.** financial; **7.** proof;
8. location; **9.** prove; **10.** embarrassing

 For additional practice with word families, have students visit *Q Online Practice*.

▶ *Listening and Speaking 3 page 137*

SPEAKING

Grammar: Past perfect (10 minutes)

1. Read the information about the past perfect aloud.

2. Check comprehension by asking questions: *When do we use the past perfect in relation to the simple past? What is the form of the past perfect?* (had + past participle) *Which adverbs is the past perfect often used with? What kind of clauses do we use the past perfect in? What are some words these clauses often begin with?*

Skill Note

Point out that many native speakers do not use the past perfect if the meaning of the sentence is clear with two simple past verbs, for example, *My parents went to bed before I got home.* Remind students that time clauses with *when* often require use of the past perfect to make the meaning clear, e.g., *My parents went to bed when I got home.* (I got home and they went to bed.) *My parents had gone to bed when I got home.* (They went to bed and then I got home.)

A (5 minutes)

1. Tell students they are going to write sentences with the past perfect. Review the first one with the class as an example.

2. Tell students to mark the sentences 1 and 2 and then write their sentences.

3. Call on volunteers to read their sentences.

Activity A Answers, p. 137
Possible answers:
2. (1, 2) I hadn't heard about the Loch Ness monster until I read the article.
3. (2, 1) We had finished hiking before it started to rain.
4. (2, 1) By the time Mari picked the phone up, It had stopped ringing.
5. (2, 1) I hadn't realized my sweater was on backwards until my sister told me.
6. (1, 2) Hilario had left his house when his mother called.
7. (1, 2) I had drunk the cup of coffee before I realized it was not mine.
8. (2, 1) Our plane had departed by the time we arrived at the airport.

▶ *Listening and Speaking 3, page 138*

B (10 minutes)

1. Tell students to complete the sentences with information that is true for them. Remind them to use the past perfect.

2. Put students in pairs to read their sentences.

3. Call on volunteers to read their sentences.

Activity B Answers, p. 138
Answers will vary. Possible answers:
1. I had lost my keys when I got home yesterday.
2. I hadn't understood lectures until I started taking this class.
3. I had turned 18 by the time I graduated from high school.
4. I had moved to the United States by the year 2000.
5. I had learned to drive before I was 21.

For additional practice with the past perfect, have students visit *Q Online Practice*.

▶ *Listening and Speaking 3, page 139*

Pronunciation:
Contractions of *had* (10 minutes)

🔊 CD2, Track 41

1. Tell students to read the information about contracted forms of *had*.

2. Check comprehension by asking: *When does the speaker join 'd to words that follow? (When those words begin with vowels sounds, l or r.) Do we use a contracted form of* had *with questions? What is the negative contracted form?*

3. Tell students to read the examples while they listen to the audio

4. Play the audio again, pausing for students to repeat.

A (10 minutes)

🔊 CD2, Track 42

1. Tell students to look at the first pair of sentences. Elicit the difference. (The verb in the first is the simple present; in the second it is the past perfect.)

2. Tell students they are going to hear only one of the sentences from each pair. Tell them to check the sentence they hear.

3. Ask students to quickly read the sentences. Elicit any questions or difficulties.

4. Play the audio while students check the correct sentences.

5. Check as a class. Play the audio again to confirm.

> **Activity A Answers, p. 139**
> **1.** He'd worked at a bookstore.
> **2.** We left when it started raining.
> **3.** They answered the questions.
> **4.** I'd eaten my lunch.
> **5.** You'd already taken the test.
> **6.** She hadn't worked there.
> **7.** It hasn't started to rain.
> **8.** Had he found it?
> **9.** Have you called Alex?

▶ *Listening and Speaking 3, page 140*

B (5 minutes)

🔊 CD2, Track 43

1. Tell students they are going to listen to the sentences again and repeat them.

2. Play the audio, pausing for students to repeat the sentences.

3. Put students in pairs. Tell them to choose either sentence from each pair to say to their partner.

4. Explain that their partner should hold up one finger if they hear the first sentence in the pair, or two if they hear the second. Tell them to change roles after one sentence from each pair has been read.

5. Monitor students' activity. Pay attention to the contracted forms of *had*.

 For additional practice of contractions with *had*, have students visit *Q Online Practice*.

Speaking Skill:
Giving a short presentation (5 minutes)

1. Direct students to read the information about giving a short presentation. Point out that it is important to introduce and organize all presentations, even short ones.

2. Check comprehension: *What phrases can you use to introduce your topic? Why should you use words and phrases to make the order of events clear? What phrases can you use to do this?*

21ˢᵀ CENTURY SKILLS

Creativity and ability to communicate are essential skills for success in one's professional and academic life in the 21st century. Facilitate students' creativity and communication by asking them to give a short presentation about a famous person who took a significant risk. Tell students to think about the following people who took risks, and choose one to talk about: Christopher Columbus, Mahatma Gandhi, Nelson Mandela, Dr. Martin Luther King, Jr., Amelia Earhart, Marie Curie, or a person of their choice. Ask them to address the following in their presentations: What did he or she risk? What made their action a risk? Would the risk they took still be considered a risk today? Was the risk worth taking? Put students in groups to give a one- or two-minute presentation to the other students.

▶ *Listening and Speaking 3, page 141*

A (10 minutes)

🔊 CD2, Track 44

1. Tell students they are going to listen to a presentation on learning Japanese. Have students read the paragraph. Elicit any questions or difficulties.

2. Play the audio while students complete the paragraph. Pause as necessary to give students time to write.

3. Put students in pairs to compare their answers. Call on volunteers to share their answers.

4. Play the audio again to clarify any difficulties.

> **Activity A Answers, p. 141**
> **1.** I'm going to talk;   **2.** By the time;   **3.** so;   **4.** so;
> **5.** Before;   **6.** By the time

B (10 minutes)

1. Keep students in pairs. Tell students to work individually to check the risks they have taken to learn English. Remind them to add ideas of their own.

2. Call on volunteers to share their own ideas.

Tip for Success

Point out it is typical to end a presentation with falling intonation to signal that the presentation has ended. Tell students that this is important so that the audience knows they may ask questions or make comments.

 For additional practice with giving a short presentation, have students visit *Q Online Practice*.

C (10 minutes)

1. Keep students in pairs. Tell them to take turns talking about the risks they checked in Activity B.

2. Remind them to use the words and phrases from the speaking skill box on page 140.

3. Encourage students to ask their partners questions to make the order of events or the reason for taking risks clear.

4. Call on volunteers to share the most interesting thing they've learned about their partner.

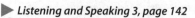 *Listening and Speaking 3, page 142*

Q Unit Assignment:
Give a short presentation

Unit Question (5 minutes)

Refer students to the ideas they discussed at the beginning of the unit about what risks are good to take. Cue students if necessary by asking specific questions about the content of the unit: *What are some of the different types of risks that people take? Why do people take these risks?*

Learning Outcome

1. Tie the unit assignment to the unit learning outcome. Say: *The outcome for this unit is to give a short presentation on a risk you have taken. This unit assignment is going to let you show your skill in giving a short presentation. Giving a short presentation is a useful skill because it allows you to share your knowledge and opinion with others. In doing so, we have the opportunity to educate others.*

2. Explain that you are going to use a rubric similar to their Self-Assessment checklist on page 144 to grade their unit assignment.

Consider the Ideas (5 minutes)

CD2, Track 45

1. Tell students they are going to listen to a woman talking about a risk she took and her reasons for taking it.

2. Tell students to look at the photos and the questions. Elicit what they think the risk is.

3. Tell students to take notes as they listen. Remind them of the features of good notes (no complete sentences, only main points, etc.).

4. Play the audio while students take notes.

5. Put students in pairs to compare their notes.

6. Check the answers to the questions as a class.

> **Consider the Ideas Answers, p. 142**
> Answers will vary. Possible answers:
> **1.** She had had a good job, a nice house, a good social life, and lots of friends.
> **2.** She risked her job and her normal life.
> **3.** Yes, she was much happier with her life after taking the risk
> **4.** She had to start over.

Prepare and Speak

Gather Ideas

A (5 minutes)

1. Direct students to write notes on similar risks in their own life. Encourage them to add any new ideas they have.

2. Point out that students should write as much information as possible since they will have the opportunity to select the most important information in the next activity.

3. Remind students not to write complete sentences.

▶ *Listening and Speaking 3, page 143*

Organize Ideas

B (10 minutes)

1. Tell students to choose one of their risks from their notes in Activity A and complete the outline.

2. Remind students not to write complete sentences, just the most important points they need to mention. Point out that they only have one minute to give their presentation so they need to be selective.

▶ *Listening and Speaking 3, page 144*

Speak

C (10–15 minutes)

1. Review the checklist on page 144. Ask students to read it. Elicit any questions.

2. Depending on the size of your class, you may wish to put students in groups to give their presentation or have students present to the entire class.

3. Remind students not to read directly from their outlines. Remind them to use appropriate phrases to introduce their topic as well as show the order of events and their reasons for taking the risk.

4. Use the unit assignment rubric on page 76 of this *Teacher's Handbook* to score each student's presentation.

5. Monitor students' performance as they present.

Alternative Unit Assignments

Assign or have students choose one of these assignments to do instead of, or in addition to, the unit assignment.

1. Do you agree with the idea that successful language learners have to be risk takers? Why or why not? Discuss your ideas with a partner or in a small group.

2. If some risks are worth taking, and others not, how can you tell the difference? Go online and research terms such as "healthy risk taking," "positive risk taking," and "benefits of risk taking" to find out about good ways to take risks. Tell a partner about your research.

 For an additional unit assignment, have students visit *Q Online Practice*.

Check and Reflect

Check

A (5 minutes)

1. Direct students to read and complete the Self-Assessment checklist.

2. Ask for a show of hands for how many students gave all or mostly yes answers.

3. Congratulate them on their success. Discuss the steps they can take if an item on the checklist was difficult for them. For example, if they had trouble with contracted forms of *had*, they can record themselves speaking and ask another student to listen to them.

Reflect

B (5 minutes)

Refer students to the learning outcome on page 125. Tell them to talk with their partners about whether they achieved the learning outcome. Elicit the answers to the unit question that students came up with at the beginning of class. Encourage them to flip through the unit as they discuss the new things they learned and new answers they may have to the unit question.

▶ *Listening and Speaking 3, page 145*

Track Your Success

1. Have students circle the words they have learned in this unit. Suggest that students go back through the unit to review any words they have forgotten.

2. Have students check the skills they have mastered. If students need more practice to feel confident about their proficiency in a skill, point out the page numbers and encourage them to review.

3. Read the learning outcome aloud. Ask students if they feel that they have met the outcome.

Unit 7   Risk

Unit Assignment Rubric

Student name: _____

Date: _____

Unit Assignment: *Give a short presentation.*

20 = Presentation element was completely successful (at least 90% of the time).
15 = Presentation element was mostly successful (at least 70% of the time).
10 = Presentation element was partially successful (at least 50% of the time).
 0 = Presentation element was not successful.

Give a short presentation	20 points	15 points	10 points	0 points
Student spoke easily (without long pauses or reading) about a risk he or she had taken and was easy to understand (spoke clearly and at a good speed).				
Student used correct past perfect verb forms.				
Student used appropriate contracted forms of *had*.				
Student used vocabulary from the unit.				
Student organized the presentation by using appropriate phrases to introduce the topic, show order of events, and reasons for behavior.				

Total points: _____

Comments:

Unit QUESTION

What do our cities say about us?

Cities

LISTENING • understanding figurative meaning
VOCABULARY • phrasal verbs
GRAMMAR • separable and inseparable phrasal verbs
PRONUNCIATION • links between consonants and vowels
SPEAKING • recapping a presentation

LEARNING OUTCOME

Give and recap a presentation highlighting what you like and dislike about a particular city.

▶ *Listening and Speaking 3, pages 146–147*

Preview the Unit

Learning Outcome

1. Ask for a volunteer to read the unit skills and then the unit learning outcome.

2. Explain: *The learning outcome is what you are expected to be able to do by the unit's end. You are going to be evaluated on how well you meet this outcome. With this in mind, you should focus on learning skills (Listening, Vocabulary, Grammar, Pronunciation, Speaking) that will support your goal of giving and recapping a presentation that highlights what you like and dislike about a particular city. This can also help you act as mentors in the classroom to help the other students meet this outcome.*

A (10 minutes)

1. Prepare students for thinking about the topic by eliciting students' opinions about the city they are in or the city that is closest to their institution of learning. Start the discussion by asking questions such as: *What do you think about the size of this city? Are there enough interesting things to do in the city? Is it an affordable city or is it very expensive?* Write students' opinions about these and other characteristics of the city on the board.

2. Put students in pairs or small groups to discuss the first four questions.

3. Call on volunteers to share their ideas with the class. Ask questions to facilitate the discussion: *What are the things about our city, or the closest city that most fit your personality? Which things do not fit your personality? What would you like to change about this city? Which city would you most like to live in?*

4. Focus students' attention on the photo. Have a volunteer describe the photo to the class. Read the question aloud.

Activity A Answers, p. 147
Possible answers:
1. The city may suit one's personality because of its size, things to do, location, character. It may not suit one's personality for the same reasons.
2. Students will have different opinions about this based on personality and previous experience.
3. The city is Paris, France's capital and largest city. It is known for museums and monuments, like the Eiffel Tower.

B (15 minutes)

1. Introduce the Unit Question, "What do our cities say about us?" Ask related information questions or questions about personal experience to help students prepare for answering the unit question, which is more abstract. *Where are many of the most famous cities located? What features do most well-known cities have in common? Do most cities look the same? How are they different?*

2. Put students in small groups and give each group a piece of poster paper and a marker.

3. Read the unit question aloud. Give students a minute to silently consider their answers to the question. Tell students to pass the paper and the marker around the group. Direct each group member to write a different answer to the question. Encourage them to help one another.

4. Ask each group to choose a reporter to read the answers to the class. Point out similarities, and differences among the answers. If answers from different groups are similar, make a group list that incorporates the answers that are similar. Post the list to refer to later in the unit.

Possible answers: The things that are popular show the people's interests. For example, if the people are interested in art, there will be a lot of museums; How crowded a city is shows how popular or important it is.

The Q Classroom

CD3, Track 02

1. Play *The Q Classroom*. Use the example from the audio to help students continue the conversation. Ask: *What kind of city do the students live in? Do they like it? Why?*

2. In the audio, students mention that people who live in a small town like a more quiet life. Elicit students' opinions as to whether this is true. If necessary, begin the discussion by mentioning reasons why people live in a place, for example, their family is there, job opportunities, etc.

▶ *Listening and Speaking 3, page 148*

C (10 minutes)

1. Tell students they are going to complete a quiz about famous cities. Ask students to read the quiz. Elicit any questions about vocabulary.

2. Explain that students should match each city with the correct description. Point out that they should look for clues in the descriptions to help them, for example, place names or geographical information.

3. Have students complete the quiz and then score themselves using check your answers. Tell them to rate their performance according to the key at the bottom of the quiz.

4. Elicit the clues that helped students if they weren't sure.

MULTILEVEL OPTION

Put lower-level students in groups to complete the task or assist them. Ask higher-level students to rank the cities based on their descriptions from most appealing to least appealing. Tell them to give specific reasons for their rankings.

D (10 minutes)

1. Put students in groups to discuss the questions.

2. Point out that they should discuss specific things that they like and dislike, as well as give reasons for their opinions. Remind them to use examples to support their opinions.

3. Call on volunteers to report their group's findings.

Students' answers may vary. Possible answers:
1. I like how many different restaurants there are. I dislike how crowded it is.
2. Hong Kong has made the biggest impression on me. It was a positive impression, because the city is so vibrant and full of life.

LISTENING

▶ *Listening and Speaking 3, page 149*

LISTENING 1: Do Cities Have Personalities?

VOCABULARY (15 minutes)

1. Direct students to read the words and their definitions. Elicit any difficulties or questions.

2. Model correct pronunciation of the words. Say each word and have students repeat.

3. Ask students to complete the sentences.

4. Put students in pairs to check their answers. Ask volunteers to read their answers. Elicit or provide corrections as necessary.

MULTILEVEL OPTION

Group lower-level students and assist them with the task. Point out the cues in the sentences that will help them to choose the correct word. Give them additional sentences to help them practice the difficult vocabulary. For example: *It is important to be aware of your **surroundings** when you are walking alone at night; The laptop computer was an **innovation** that made life much easier for businesspeople.*

Have higher-level students complete the activity individually and then compare answers with a partner. Tell the pairs to write an additional sample sentence for each word. Have volunteers write one of their sentences on the board. Correct the sentences with the whole class, focusing on the use of the vocabulary word rather than other grammatical issues.

Vocabulary Answers, p. 149
1. region; **2.** surroundings; **3.** innovation;
4. mobile; **5.** agreeable; **6.** satisfy; **7.** attract;
8. conscientious; **9.** hand in hand; **10.** tend to

 For additional practice with the vocabulary, have students visit *Q Online Practice*.

PREVIEW LISTENING 1 (5 minutes)

1. Direct students to read the information. Ask: *Do you think cities have personalities? Why or why not?*

2. Ask students whether they think people with similar personalities choose to live in the same place. Tell them to check their answer after they listen.

> **Preview Listening 1 Answer, p. 150**
> Students' answers will vary. In the listening, the argument is made that people with similar personalities do choose to live in the same place.

Listening 1 Background Note

Professor Richard Florida was born in the United States in 1957. He earned a PhD from Columbia University in 1986. His research is on urban regeneration, specifically the rise of a creative class. The creative class refers to individuals who are innovative, creative, and highly sought after by businesses.

LISTEN FOR MAIN IDEAS (5 minutes)

 CD3, Track 3

1. Explain that students are going to listen to the report and write *T* or *F* next to the statements.

2. Ask students to read the information. Elicit any questions or difficulties.

3. Play the audio and have students complete the activity individually.

4. Elicit the answers from the class.

> **Main Idea Answers, p. 150**
> **1.** F; **2.** T; **3.** T; **4.** F; **5.** T; **6.** F

Tip for Success

Point out that it is important to listen for opinions. Simply hearing the word *think* or *believe* does not indicate that the speaker holds that opinion since the speaker may be introducing someone else's ideas. As a result, it is important to pay attention for such introductions.

LISTEN FOR DETAILS (10 minutes)

 CD3, Track 4

1. Direct students to read the names of the cities and the kinds of work before they listen again. Elicit any questions about them.

2. As you play the audio, have students listen and match the cities with the kinds of work.

3. Have students compare their answers with a partner.

4. Replay the audio so that the partners can check their answers.

5. Go over the answers with the class.

> **Listen for Details Answers, p. 151**
> **1.** d; **2.** e; **3.** b; **4.** f; **5.** a; **6.** c

> **web** For additional practice with listening comprehension, have students visit *Q Online Practice*.

Expansion Activity: Personality Factors (10 minutes)

1. Put students into pairs or groups.

2. Remind them that in Listening 1, they heard about how a city's personality can be related to the people that live there.

3. Ask students to think about other thing that may affect a city's personality, for instance, the weather, or an important part of its history.

4. Have students discuss their ideas in their groups.

5. Elicit answers from volunteers.

Q WHAT DO YOU THINK? (10 minutes)

1. Ask students to read the questions and reflect on their answers.

2. Seat students in small groups and assign roles: a group leader to make sure everyone contributes, a note-taker to record the group's ideas, a reporter to share the group's ideas with the class, and a timekeeper to watch the clock.

3. Give students five minutes to discuss the questions. Call time if conversations are winding down. Allow them an extra minute or two if necessary.

4. Call on each group's reporter to share ideas with the class.

Answers will vary. Possible answers:
1. Yes, because people want to be around like-minded thinkers; No, because many cities are full of a variety of personalities.
2. Student may talk about a city in their native country that is well-known for a particular industry.

Learning Outcome

Use the learning outcome to frame the purpose and relevance of Listening 1. Ask: *What did you learn from Listening 1 that prepares you to give a short presentation highlighting what you like and dislike about a particular city? What did you learn that will help you recap that presentation?*

▶ *Listening and Speaking 3, page 152*

Listening Skill: Understanding figurative meaning (10 minutes)

CD3, Track 5

1. Ask students to read the information about understanding figurative meaning and the first two examples. Elicit any difficulties or questions.
2. Check comprehension by asking questions: *What is the difference between literal and figurative language?*
3. Tell students to follow along in their books while they listen to the excerpt of figurative language from Listening 1.
4. Ask students to read the explanation after the excerpt.
5. Check comprehension by asking questions: *Why is the use of the words* magnets *and* spark *figurative? Why is it important to be able to understand figurative language?*

A (10 minutes)

1. Ask students to read the sentences in the box. Point out that the words in bold are used with their literal meanings.
2. Tell students they are going to read the sentences in which the words in bold are used figuratively and then complete the sentence that follows. Point out that the sentence asks them to identify the things that are compared between the literal and figurative meanings.
3. Do the first one as an example.

4. Students complete the sentences individually.
5. Put students in pairs to check their answers. Check the answers as a class.

> **Activity A Answers, p. 152**
> **2.** body; **3.** rocket; **4.** plant

▶ *Listening and Speaking 3, page 153*

B (10 minutes)

CD3, Track 6

1. Tell students they are going to listen and complete the sentences with the word they hear. Point out that after they listen, they are then going to complete the comparisons.
2. Ask students to read the sentences. Elicit any questions or difficulties.
3. Play the audio while students complete the sentences individually.
4. Tell students to complete the comparisons individually.
5. Put students in pairs to share their answers. Elicit the answers from the class.

> **Activity B Answers, p. 153**
> **1.** heart, body; **2.** seed, plant;
> **3.** ate, person or animal; **4.** flew, a bird or a plane

 For additional practice with figurative language, have students visit *Q Online Practice*.

LISTENING 2:
Buenos Aires, Beijing, and Dubai

VOCABULARY (10 minutes)

1. Pronounce the words in bold and have students repeat them.
2. Put students in pairs to circle the answer that best matches the meaning of the word in bold.
3. Encourage students to use their knowledge of prefixes, suffixes, and roots. Also encourage them to use a dictionary.
4. Ask volunteers to share their answers.

> **Vocabulary Answers, p. 153**
> **1.** man-made; **2.** honor; **3.** personality;
> **4.** honest; **5.** exciting; **6.** exact;
> **7.** give; **8.** uncover; **9.** modernize;
> **10.** belief

Group lower-level students and assist them with the task. Point out the cues in the words that will help them to understand the word's meaning, for example the word **lively** is related to the word *alive*, which is similar to *full of life*. Give them additional sentences to help them practice the difficult vocabulary. For example: I *like working with people who are* **direct** *because I know how they feel. I don't know the* **precise** *time that I put the food in the oven.*

Have higher-level students complete the activity individually and then compare answers with a partner. Tell the pairs to write a sentence for each word. Have volunteers write one of their sentences on the board. Correct the sentences with the whole class, focusing on the use of the vocabulary word rather than other grammatical issues.

For additional practice with the vocabulary, have students visit *Q Online Practice.*

▶ *Listening and Speaking 3, page 154*

PREVIEW LISTENING 2 (5 minutes)

1. Tell students they are going to listen to descriptions of Buenos Aires, Beijing, and Dubai. Elicit what students know about these cities, including where they are located and what they are famous for.

2. Ask students to look at the photos of the cities and give their opinions about them.

Listening 2 Background Note

Buenos Aires is the largest city and capital of Argentina. It is also the second largest city in South America, after Sao Paulo, Brazil. Buenos Aires is known for the European flavor in its architecture and culture. It is sometimes referred to as the Paris of South America.

Beijing, located in the northeast of China, is the capital of that country. Once known as Peking, Beijing is one of the largest cities in the world. It is a modern, 21st-century city with skyscrapers and modern conveniences, but there is evidence of its traditional past in its imperial Chinese architecture, such as the Forbidden City complex.

Dubai is one of the seven Emirates, or kingdoms, that form the United Arab Emirates. Dubai has the largest population and the second largest area, after Abu Dhabi, in the United Arab Emirates. Dubai is known for its wealth, stemming from banking and business related to the oil industry.

LISTEN FOR MAIN IDEAS (15 minutes)

◉ CD3, Track 7

1. Explain that students will listen and write the letters for two of the descriptions next to each city.

2. Ask students to read the descriptions. Elicit any difficulties with vocabulary or concepts.

3. Play the audio while students work individually.

4. Call on volunteers to share their answers.

> **Listen for Main Idea Answers, p. 154**
> **1.** c, e;   **2.** d, f;   **3.** a, b

▶ *Listening and Speaking 3, page 155*

LISTEN FOR DETAILS (10 minutes)

◉ CD3, Track 8

1. Tell students they are going to listen again and write the abbreviation for one of the three cities next to the each detail. Ask them to read the details. Elicit any questions or difficulties.

2. Play the audio while students write the abbreviations.

3. Have students compare answers with a partner.

4. Go over the answers with the class.

> **Listen for Details Answers, p. 155**
> **1.** BA;   **2.** D;   **3.** B;   **4.** BA;
> **5.** B;   **6.** D;   **7.** BA;   **8.** D

For additional practice with listening comprehension, have students visit *Q Online Practice.*

WHAT DO YOU THINK?

A (10 minutes)

1. Ask students to read the questions and reflect on their answers.

2. Seat students in small groups and assign roles: a group leader to make sure everyone contributes, a note-taker to record the group's ideas, a reporter to share the group's ideas with the class, and a timekeeper to watch the clock.

3. Give students five minutes to discuss the questions. Call time if conversations are winding down. Allow them an extra minute or two if necessary.

4. Call on each group's reporter to share ideas with the class.

Students' answers will vary. Possible answers:
1. Beijing, because it is always changing. I would never get bored.
2. Students should be able to give reasons for their answers.

B (10 minutes)

1. Have students continue working their small groups to discuss the questions in Activity B. Tell them to choose a new leader, recorder, reporter, and timekeeper.

2. For question 1, recap Professor Florida's points about the personality of individuals and the cities they live in from Listening 1.

3. Call on the new reporter to share the group's answers to the questions.

Activity B Answers, p. 155
Answers will vary. Possible answers:
1. Yes, cities do have personalities and the people there often have the same personality as the city; No, there are too many different people living in a city for it to just have one personality.
2. Students should be able to give reasons and examples for their answers.

Tip for Critical Thinking (1 minute)

Read the tip aloud. Point out that relating information to one's own experience is also a good way to analyze information. By relating information to your own experience, you are better able to see the differences and similarities between your experience and the new information.

Critical Q: Expansion Activity

Relating information to aid analysis

1. Give students three minutes to brainstorm the characteristics of their favorite city or a city they know well, including fun things to do, types of industries or jobs, etc. If students are from the same city, ask them to choose another city they have visited and know well.

2. Put students in small groups. Ask each student to read the characteristics of the city they thought about while the others take notes. Remind students they are not giving a presentation, just reading their information.

3. Tell the students to relate the information they heard about each city to their own experiences and form an opinion about which city they would most like to live in and why.

4. Have students share their opinions in their groups, including the experiences from their own lives that they related the new information to in order to form their opinion.

5. Call on volunteers to share their opinions and reasons with the class.

Learning Outcome

Use the learning outcome to frame the purpose and relevance of Listenings 1 and 2 and the Critical Q activity of relating information. Ask: *What did you learn from the listenings that prepares you to give a presentation about what you like about a city? What did you learn that will help you given a presentation about what you dislike about a city?*

▶ *Listening and Speaking 3, page 156*

Vocabulary Skill: Phrasal verbs (5 minutes)

1. Direct students to read the information in the first paragraph silently.

2. Check comprehension: *What is a phrasal verb? What is a particle? Do phrasal verbs have the same meaning that the verb and the particle do individually?*

3. Ask students to read the example and the remaining information. Elicit how the verb *look into* in the first example sentence differs from *look into* in the second example sentence. (In the first sentence, both are used literally, i.e., gazing into the room. In the second they are used together and create a figurative meaning for *investigate*.).

4. Elicit any questions or difficulties about the information.

A (10 minutes)

1. Tell students to read the sentences and circle the answer that best matches the meaning of the bold phrase. Remind students that they should think about the context, not the meaning of the words by themselves.

2. Have students work individually to choose their answers. Then tell students to check sentences which have phrasal verbs.

3. Put students in pairs to compare their answers.

4. Go over the answers with the class.

Activity A Answers, p. 156
1. a; 2. b; 3. b; 4. a; 5. a;
6. b; 7. b; 8. a; 9. b; 10. a
Sentences with phrasal verbs: 2, 4, 6, 7, 9

▶ *Listening and Speaking 3, page 157*

B (5 minutes)

1. Keep students in pairs, but have students do the activity individually. Point out that they may have to change the tense of some of the phrasal verbs.

2. Have students compare their answers with their partner. Call on volunteers to read their answers.

Activity B Answers, p. 157
1. came to;   **2.** go out;   **3.** bring up;
4. deal with;   **5.** turn into

 For additional practice with phrasal verbs have students visit *Q Online Practice.*

▶ *Listening and Speaking 3, page 158*

SPEAKING

Grammar: Separable and inseparable phrasal verbs (10 minutes)

1. Read the first two paragraphs about phrasal verbs and the examples aloud.

2. Check comprehension by asking questions: *What is a separable phrasal verb? What separates the parts of the phrasal verb?*

3. Read aloud the remaining information on separable phrasal verbs and object pronouns as well as the examples.

4. Ask students to read the list of separable phrasal verbs silently. Elicit any questions about meaning.

5. Check comprehension by asking questions: *Why are the sentences with the red X incorrect? How can we make these two sentences correct?* (By using the noun instead of the pronoun.)

6. Read the information and examples of inseparable phrasal verbs aloud.

7. Check comprehension by asking questions: *Why are the sentences with the red X incorrect?*

8. Ask students to read the list of inseparable phrasal verbs silently. Elicit any questions about meaning.

Skill Note

Point out that phrasal verbs are extremely common in spoken English. Explain that students need to pay special attention to separable phrasal verbs when they are used with object pronouns because they may not be listening for a phrasal verb. As a result, they may miss the particle of the phrasal verb and consequently, they may fail to notice the speaker's figurative use of language. This can lead to miscommunication.

▶ *Listening and Speaking 3, page 159*

A (5 minutes)

1. Tell students they are going to rewrite the sentences with object pronouns. Review the first one with the class as an example.

2. Review the object pronouns if necessary.

3. Ask students to write their sentences individually.

4. Put students in pairs to check their sentences.

5. Call on volunteers to read their sentences aloud.

Activity A Answers, p. 159
2. We usually run into her at the gym.
3. Linda and Victor talked it over before class.
4. Hong hasn't gotten over it yet.
5. Will you look after it while I'm in São Paulo?
6. I didn't put them away after dinner.

B (10 minutes)

1. Tell students to write answers to the questions, using the object pronouns when possible. Remind students to review the rules for object pronouns and separable phrasal verbs on page 158.

2. Tell students to write their answers individually.

3. Put students in pairs to take turns asking and answering the questions. Tell students to correct any mistakes their partner may have made.

4. Call on volunteers to read their answers aloud.

Activity B Answers, p. 159
Answers may vary. Possible answers:
1. I looked them up in my dictionary.
2. I handed it in to the teacher.
3. My teacher pointed it out to us.
4. No, we didn't go over it.
5. Yes, I talked it over with my partner.

 For additional practice with separable and inseparable phrasal verbs, have students visit *Q Online Practice.*

Pronunciation: Links between consonants and vowels (10 minutes)

🔊 CD3, Track 9

1. Ask students to read the information on linking between consonants and vowels.

2. Elicit the vowels and their sounds.

3. Check comprehension by asking: *Why is linking common in phrasal verbs? What does it mean when words are linked?* (There is no pause between them.)

4. Tell students to read the examples while they listen to the audio. Elicit why *come over* is linked despite the word *come* ending in a vowel (Because the final sound is a consonant, not a vowel.)

5. Play the audio again, pausing for students to repeat.

A (5 minutes)

🔊 CD3, Track 10

1. Tell students to read the sentences and connect the words they think will be linked.

2. Play the audio while students check their links.

3. Elicit any difficulties or questions students had about identifying the linked words.

4. Play the audio again, pausing for students to repeat.

B (10 minutes)

1. Tell students they are going to practice linking by asking and answering questions.

2. Ask students to read the questions. Elicit any questions or difficulties in meaning.

3. Tell students to connect the words that should be linked. Check the words for linking as a class.

4. Put students in pairs. Tell them to take turns asking and answering the questions. Remind them to listen for the linking in their partner's speech.

5. Monitor students' activity. Pay attention to the linking between consonants and vowels, especially on the phrasal verbs.

 For additional practice with linking between consonants and vowels, have students visit *Q Online Practice*.

Speaking Skill: Recapping a presentation (5 minutes)

1. Direct students to read the information about recapping a presentation.

2. Check comprehension: *Why is it important to recap or summarize? How long should the recap be? What are some phrases you can use to recap a presentation?*

21ST CENTURY SKILLS

Being able to summarize effectively is a useful skill for one's professional and academic work. Students may find that in the workplace, they have a limited amount of time to convey the essential information to managers, teams, or customers. Similarly, in their academic work, students will often be required to read extensively but present only the most important information to their professors and classmates. In order to prepare students to effectively summarize, give them extensive practice. Assign speaking summaries throughout the course or term. Tell students to summarize a program they have watched or a lecture they have heard. Give them one minute to summarize the plot or the most important points. You may wish to tailor the activity to students' abilities; for example, asking lower-level students to summarize a half-hour show while having higher-level students summarize longer documentaries, movies, or lectures.

A (10 minutes)

🔊 CD3, Track 11

1. Tell students they are going to listen to a presentation about the American city of Charlotte. Explain that they should take notes in the T-chart about the advantages and disadvantages of the city.

2. Elicit the features of good notes (do not use complete sentences, use abbreviations, etc.).

3. Play the audio while students take notes. Pause as necessary to give students time to write.

4. Do not check answers until students have done Activities B and C.

B (10 minutes)

1. Put students in pairs. Tell them to take turns summarizing the advantages and disadvantages according to their T-charts.

2. Remind them not to simply read their notes. Ask them to present the advantages and disadvantages using the notes only as a guide.

3. Do not elicit any answers until students have had a chance to complete Activity C.

C (10 minutes)

CD3, Track 12

1. Keep students in pairs. Tell them they will check the information in their charts while they listen to a summary of the presentation.

2. Play the audio while students check their notes.

3. Write a T-chart on the board. Call on volunteers to share their information from their T-charts. Write it on the board. Check the information as a class.

Activity A, B, C Answers, p. 161

Advantages	Disadvantages
Pretty Clean Friendly people Becoming more diverse	A little quiet Not as much to do as in Boston Fewer cultural activities Fewer places to eat Fewer creative people

 For additional practice on recapping a presentation, have students visit *Q Online Practice*.

▶ *Listening and Speaking 3, page 162*

Unit Assignment:
Give and recap a presentation

Unit Question (5 minutes)

Refer students to the ideas they discussed at the beginning of the unit about what our cities say about us. Cue students if necessary by asking specific questions about the content of the unit: *Why do some people believe that cities have personalities? What makes a city interesting?*

Learning Outcome

1. Tie the unit assignment to the unit learning outcome. Say: *The outcome for this unit is to give a short presentation highlighting what you like and dislike about a particular city and then recap. This unit assignment is going to let you show your skill in giving and recapping a short presentation. Recapping a short presentation is a useful skill because it allows you to emphasize the most*

important points of your presentation. In doing so, we have the opportunity to persuade others and communicate information effectively.

2. Explain that you are going to use a rubric similar to their Self-Assessment checklist on page 164 to grade their unit assignment.

Consider the Ideas (5 minutes)

1. Tell students to read the list of things they might consider when choosing where to live. Have them circle the three things that are most important to them.

2. Put students in pairs to discuss their answers and reasons.

3. Conduct a quick class survey by asking for a show of hands for each of the things in the chart.

Prepare and Speak

Gather Ideas

A (5 minutes)

1. Direct students to brainstorm a list of things they like and don't like about a city they know well.

2. Point out that students should try to list as many things as they can.

3. Remind students to write the name of the city.

▶ *Listening and Speaking 3, page 163*

Organize Ideas

B (10 minutes)

1. Tell students to choose the three likes and dislikes that they feel most strongly about to complete the sentences in the outline.

2. Remind students to write the name of the city.

3. Ask students to create a statement that recaps their likes and dislikes.

Tip for Success (1 minute)

Read the tip aloud. Point out that the recap may not make an impact on the audience if the audience isn't ready for it. Explain that this is why the pause is necessary.

Speak

C (10–15 minutes)

1. Review the checklist on page 164. Ask students to read it. Elicit any questions.

2. Depending on the size of your class, you may wish to put students in groups to give their presentation or have students present to the entire class.

3. Remind students not to read directly from their outlines. Remind them to link words' ending consonants to those beginning with vowels. Also remind them to pause before their recap statement.

4. Use the unit assignment rubric on page 87 of this *Teacher's Handbook* to score each student's presentation.

5. Monitor students' performance as they present.

Alternative Unit Assignments

Assign or have students choose one of these assignments to do instead of, or in addition, to the unit assignment.

1. Compare the "personalities" of two cities. Tell a partner or group the advantages and disadvantages of each.

2. Choose one of the cities mentioned in the unit, or another city that interests you. Research two opposing opinions about the city and present them to your classmates.

 For an additional unit assignment, have students visit *Q Online Practice*.

▶ *Listening and Speaking 3, page 164*

Check and Reflect

Check

A (5 minutes)

1. Direct students to read and complete the Self-Assessment checklist.

2. Ask for a show of hands for how many students gave all or mostly yes answers.

3. Congratulate them on their success. Discuss the steps they can take if an item on the checklist was difficult for them. For example, if they had trouble with linking, they can record themselves speaking and ask another student to listen to them.

Reflect

B (5 minutes)

Refer students to the learning outcome on page 147. Tell them to talk with their partners about whether they achieved the learning outcome. Elicit the answers to the unit question that students came up with at the beginning of class. Encourage them to flip through the unit as they discuss the new things they learned and new answers they may have to the unit question.

▶ *Listening and Speaking 3, page 165*

Track Your Success

1. Have students circle the words they have learned in this unit. Suggest that students go back through the unit to review any words they have forgotten.

2. Have students check the skills they have mastered. If students need more practice to feel confident about their proficiency in a skill, point out the page numbers and encourage them to review.

3. Read the learning outcome aloud. Ask students if they feel that they have met the outcome.

Unit Assignment Rubric

Student name: _____

Date: _____

Unit Assignment: *Give and recap a presentation.*

20 = Presentation element was completely successful (at least 90% of the time).
15 = Presentation element was mostly successful (at least 70% of the time).
10 = Presentation element was partially successful (at least 50% of the time).
 0 = Presentation element was not successful.

Give and recap a presentation	20 points	15 points	10 points	0 points
Student spoke easily (without long pauses or reading) about what he/she liked and disliked about a city and was easy to understand (spoke clearly and at a good speed).				
Student used correct figurative language or phrasal verbs.				
Student linked words ending in consonants to those beginning with vowels.				
Student used vocabulary from the unit.				
Student had an appropriate recap statement and paused before delivery of it.				

Total points: _____

Comments:

9

Unit QUESTION
Can money buy happiness?

Money

LISTENING • listening for signposts
VOCABULARY • using the dictionary
GRAMMAR • types of sentences
PRONUNCIATION • intonation in different types of sentences
SPEAKING • agreeing and disagreeing

LEARNING OUTCOME

Participate in a group discussion evaluating the influence money has on happiness.

▶ *Listening and Speaking 3, pages 166–167*

Preview the Unit

Learning Outcome

1. Ask for a volunteer to read the unit skills and then the unit learning outcome.

2. Explain: *The learning outcome is what you are expected to be able to do by the unit's end. You are going to be evaluated on how well you meet this outcome. With this in mind, you should focus on learning skills (Listening, Vocabulary, Grammar, Pronunciation, Speaking) that will support your goal of participating in a group discussion evaluating the influence money has on happiness. This can also help you act as mentors in the classroom to help the other students meet this outcome.*

A (10 minutes)

1. Prepare students for thinking about the topic by eliciting a class definition of *happiness*. Start the discussion by asking questions such as: *What does happiness mean to you? Is a happy person happy all the time?* Write students' opinions on the board. Accept all answers.

2. Put students in pairs or small groups to discuss the first four questions.

3. Call on volunteers to share their ideas with the class. Ask questions to facilitate the discussion: *Are people with more money happier in general? Is it harder to make friends if you have a lot of money? Why or why not? What things can money buy that you absolutely need?* (housing, food, health care, transportation, education, etc.) *Are you happy when you have enough money to buy these things?*

4. Focus students' attention on the photo. Have a volunteer describe the photo to the class. Read the questions aloud.

Activity A Answers, p. 167

1. Students may say that people only need enough money to cover their basic needs, e.g., food, clothing, shelter, medical care, education costs, or they may say people need substantially more than this to be happy.

2. Students may have different opinions about whether more money would make them happier based on how much money they currently have and / or what their lives are like now.

3. Students may think the people are happy because they are obviously wealthy, or they may wonder about other factors in the people's lives, e.g., quality of personal relationships, amount of time available to enjoy the nice house, etc.

B (15 minutes)

1. Introduce the Unit Question, "Can money buy happiness?" Ask related information questions about personal experience to help students prepare for answering the Unit Question, which is more abstract. *What are some things money can't buy? What are some things that money can help a person do? Does having money make people kinder or friendlier, or does it make them impatient or rude? Why do you think so?*

2. Read the Unit Question aloud. Give students a minute to silently consider their answer to the question and supporting details.

3. Write *Advantages of having money* and *Disadvantages of having money* at the top of two sheets of poster paper. Say, *What are the advantages of having a lot of money? What are the disadvantages of having a lot of money?*

4. Elicit student answers. Write them under the correct heading. Post the lists to refer to later in the unit.

Activity B Answers, p. 167

Possible answers: Money cannot buy happiness because happiness is generated internally, from being content with one's life, surroundings, and choices; Money cannot buy happiness because happiness has to come from inside. People can have money and still be miserable; Money can't make people happy on the inside.

The Q Classroom

CD3, Track 13

1. Play *The Q Classroom*. Use the example from the audio to help students continue the conversation. Ask: *What things did the students mention they would do if they had more money? According to Felix, what is something money can't buy?*

▶ *Listening and Speaking 3, page 168*

C (10 minutes)

1. Tell students they are going to complete a questionnaire about their priorities. Ask students to read the questionnaire. Elicit any questions about vocabulary.

2. Explain that students should rank the expenses in order of importance with 1 being the most important and 10 being the least.

MULTILEVEL OPTION

Put lower-level students in groups to complete the task or assist them. Ask higher-level students to rank the expenses and then divide the one million dollars between them. Tell them to be prepared then justify their selections.

D (10 minutes)

1. Put students in pairs to discuss their choices.

2. Point out that they should discuss the reasons for their opinions. Remind them to use examples to support their opinions.

3. Call on volunteers to report their partner's top choice and reasons for it.

E (10 minutes)

1. Keep students in pairs. Tell them to write the three things in life that make them the happiest.

2. Ask students to compare their list to the top three things they listed in Activity C. Tell them to discuss with their partners how their list relates to the list in Activity C.

3. Call on volunteers to share which list makes them happier and why.

Activity E Answers, p. 168

Students' answers will vary. Students should support their answers with reasons.

LISTENING

▶ *Listening and Speaking 3, page 169*

LISTENING 1: Sudden Wealth

VOCABULARY (15 minutes)

1. Direct students to read the words and their definitions. Elicit any difficulties or questions.

2. Model correct pronunciation of the words. Say each word and have students repeat.

3. Ask students to complete the paragraph.

4. Put students in pairs to check their answers.

5. Ask volunteers to read their answers.

MULTILEVEL OPTION

Group lower-level students and assist them with the task. Point out the cues in the sentences that will help them to choose the correct word. Give them additional sentences to help them practice the difficult vocabulary. For example: *I can't **get used to** having classes in the morning because I have always had them in the afternoon; The company saw a **dramatic** decrease in sales. Sales were at their lowest level ever.*

Have higher-level students complete the activity individually and then compare answers with a partner. Tell the pairs to write an additional sample sentence for each word. Have volunteers write one of their sentences on the board. Correct the sentences with the whole class, focusing on the use of the vocabulary word rather than other grammatical issues.

Vocabulary Answers, p. 169

1. acquire; **2.** inherit; **3.** pleasure;
4. immediate; **5.** dramatic; **6.** circumstances;
7. complicated; **8.** destructive; **9.** get/had used to;
10. wear off

 For additional practice with the vocabulary, have students visit *Q Online Practice*.

▶ *Listening and Speaking 3, page 170*

PREVIEW LISTENING 1 (5 minutes)

1. Direct students to read the information. Ask: *What are some ways that someone might become wealthy suddenly?*

2. Ask students to check the topics they think the article will discuss. Point out they can check more than one. Tell them to check their answers after they listen.

   Preview Listening 1 Answer, p. 170
   Students' answers will vary. In the listening, all three of the topics are touched on.

Listening 1 Background Note

In the United States, it is possible to become wealthy suddenly through a variety of circumstances, including inheritance, or a risky investment.

LISTEN FOR MAIN IDEAS (5 minutes)

CD3, Track 14

1. Explain that students are going to listen to the article and write *T* or *F* next to the statements.

2. Ask students to read the information. Elicit any questions or difficulties about them.

3. Play the audio and have students write *T* or *F* individually. Elicit the answers from the class.

   Main Ideas Answers, p. 170
   1. T; **2.** F; **3.** T; **4.** T; **5.** F; **6.** F

Tip for Success (1 minute)

Point out that talks sometimes begin with a question. This often indicates the speaker's main topic. These questions also serve as a hook to interest listeners in the topic. If listeners feel that their answer is in agreement with the speaker's answer they are likely to listen. Conversely, if the listeners' answer differs from what they hear, they may be curious to find out why.

▶ *Listening and Speaking 3, page 171*

LISTEN FOR DETAILS (15 minutes)

CD3, Track 15

1. Ask students to read the three main points listed in the outline. Tell them they are going to listen again and write two examples for each main point.

2. Play the audio while students list the examples. Pause as necessary to give students a chance to write.

3. Have students compare their answers with a partner.

4. Replay the audio so that the partners can check their answers. Go over the answers with the class.

Listen for Details Answers, p. 171
Answers may vary. Possible answers:

Effect on our brain (list any two)	Immediate effect is pleasure Effect wears off Have to buy more to get same pleasure
Effect on relationships (list any two)	Too many people want something from you People don't understand your stress May be alone, lose support
Effect on emotions (list any two)	Negative emotions: fear, shame, guilt, anxiety Can lead to bad decisions If inherited, can complicate emotions

 For additional practice with listening comprehension, have students visit *Q Online Practice.*

WHAT DO YOU THINK? (10 minutes)

1. Ask students to read the questions and reflect on their answers.

2. Seat students in small groups and assign roles: a group leader to make sure everyone contributes, a note-taker to record the group's ideas, a reporter to share the group's ideas with the class, and a timekeeper to watch the clock.

3. Give students five minutes to discuss the questions. Call time if conversations are winding down. Allow them an extra minute or two if necessary.

4. Call on each group's reporter to share ideas with the class.

   What Do You Think? Answers, p. 171
   Students' answers will vary. Possible Answers:
   1. Effects on our relationships because my friendships are very important to me.
   2. A friend inherited money and was able to pay off her loans. That made her happier.
   3. If someone is struggling to afford necessities, like food and shelter, sudden wealth would make them happier.

Learning Outcome

Use the learning outcome to frame the purpose and relevance of Listening 1. Ask: *What did you learn from Listening 1 that prepares you participate in a discussion about the impact of money on happiness? What did you learn that will help you evaluate the influence of money on happiness?*

 Listening and Speaking 3, page 172

Listening Skill:
Listening for signposts (5 minutes)

🔊 CD3, Track 16

1. Ask students to read the information about listening for signposts. Elicit any difficulties or questions.

2. Check comprehension by asking questions: *What are signposts? What do they help us do?*

3. Tell students to follow along in their books while they listen to the examples of signposts from Listening 1.

4. Check comprehension by asking questions: *Which phrases can you use at the start? Where do you use phrases such as* in conclusion *and* in summary?

A (10 minutes)
🔊 CD3, Track 17

1. Ask students to read the interview and predict what kind of signposts they will hear for each item. Elicit their answers and reasons.

2. Play the audio while students write the signposting phrases individually.

3. Put students in pairs to check their answers. Check the answers as a class, confirming whether students' predictions were correct.

> **Activity A Answers, p. 172**
> **1.** in the beginning;   **2.** then;   **3.** Before that;
> **4.** Finally;   **5.** First;   **6.** Next;   **7.** After that

 Listening and Speaking 3, page 173

B (10 minutes)

1. Tell students that they are going to answer the questions using signposts. Point out that they should write complete sentences.

2. Have students write their responses individually.

3. Put students in pairs to take turns asking and answering the questions. Ask students to identify their partner's signposts.

4. Call on volunteers to share their answers with the class.

> **Activity B Answers, p. 173**
> Possible answers:
> **2.** In the beginning, she didn't believe it.
> **3.** First, she paid off her credit card debt.
> **4.** After that, she sent her son to college.
> **5.** In the immediate future, she's going to go to Paris.
> **6.** She's thinking of going back to school next.

 For additional practice with signposting, have students visit *Q Online Practice*.

 Listening and Speaking 3, page 174

LISTENING 2: Happiness Breeds Success... **and Money!**

VOCABULARY (10 minutes)

1. Pronounce the words in bold and have students repeat them.

2. Ask students to read the sentences. Elicit any questions or difficulties.

3. Tell students to write the words in bold next to the correct definition.

> **Vocabulary Answers, p. 174**
> **a.** independence;   **b.** wholly;   **c.** demonstrate;
> **d.** analysis;   **e.** burn out;   **f.** conduct;
> **g.** associated with;   **h.** outcome;   **i.** persuasive;
> **j.** somewhat

> **MULTILEVEL OPTION**
>
> Group lower-level students and assist them with the task. Point out the cues in the words that will help them to understand the word's meaning, for example the word **wholly** is related to the word *whole*, which means complete. The ending *-ly* usually indicates an adverb. Therefore, **wholly** is an adverb meaning completely. Give them additional sentences to help them practice the difficult vocabulary.
>
> Have higher-level students complete the activity individually and then compare answers with a partner. Tell the pairs to write a sentence for each word. Have volunteers write one of their sentences on the board. Correct the sentences with the whole class, focusing on the use of the vocabulary word rather than other grammatical issues.

 For additional practice with the vocabulary, have students visit *Q Online Practice*.

Listening and Speaking 3, page 175

PREVIEW LISTENING 2 (5 minutes)

1. Direct students to read the information. Ask: *What have our investigations into the relationship between money and happiness revealed so far?*

2. Ask students to check the things they think the researcher will say. Point out that they can check more than one. Tell them to check their answers after they listen.

Preview Listening 2 Answer, p. 175
Students' answers will vary. In the listening, the researcher says that happiness can lead to money.

Listening 2 Background Note

Dr. Sonja Lyubomirsky is a professor in the Department of Psychology at the University of California Riverside. She is also the author of a book entitled *The How of Happiness*, which presents research-based strategies to increase one's happiness. She is also an associate editor of the *Journal of Positive Psychology*.

LISTEN FOR MAIN IDEAS (5 minutes)

CD3, Track 18

1. Tell students they will listen to the interview with Dr. Lyubomirsky. Explain that they should circle the correct answer for each item.

2. Ask students to read the sentences. Elicit any difficulties with vocabulary or concepts.

3. Play the audio while students work individually.

4. Call on volunteers to share their answers.

Listen for Main Idea Answers, p. 175
1. b; **2.** c; **3.** b; **4.** a; **5.** c

Listening and Speaking 3, page 176

LISTEN FOR DETAILS (5 minutes)

CD3, Track 19

1. Tell students they are going to listen again and write *T* or *F* for each sentence.

2. Ask students to read the sentences. Elicit any questions or difficulties.

3. Play the audio while students do the activity individually. Go over the answers with the class.

Listen for Details Answers, p. 176
1. F; **2.** T; **3.** T; **4.** F; **5.** F; **6.** T

 For additional practice with listening comprehension, have students visit *Q Online Practice*.

WHAT DO YOU THINK?

A (10 minutes)

1. Ask students to read the questions and reflect on their answers.

2. Seat students in small groups and assign roles: a group leader to make sure everyone contributes, a note-taker to record the group's ideas, a reporter to share the group's ideas with the class, and a timekeeper to watch the clock.

3. Give students five minutes to discuss the questions. Call time if conversations are winding down. Allow them an extra minute or two if necessary.

4. Call on each group's reporter to share ideas with the class.

Activity A Answers, p. 176
Students' answers will vary. Possible answers:
1. Students should support their opinions with reasons.
2. Happy people are often more positive and friendlier, which makes people want to work with them.

B (10 minutes)

1. Have students continue working their small groups to discuss the questions in activity B. Tell them to choose a new leader, recorder, reporter, and timekeeper.

2. For question 1, recap the main points from the listening. Ask: *What did we learn about people who acquire sudden wealth? How is acquiring sudden wealth different from what Professor Lyubomirsky talked about?*

3. Call on the new reporter to share the group's answers to the questions.

Activity B Answers, p. 176
Possible answers: **1.** People who acquire sudden wealth are unprepared for it and it majorly changes their lives. On the other hand, people who are happy in their work tend to earn more money and are not adversely affected by this.
2. Students should support their answers with reasons.

Tip for Critical Thinking (1 minute)

Read the tip aloud. Point out that choosing between two things requires us to evaluate the benefits and drawbacks. One way that we do this is by relating those benefits and drawbacks to our knowledge and personal experience.

Critical Q: Expansion Activity

Assessing Benefits and Drawbacks

1. Present students with a choice: They can have a job doing something boring or in a field they don't like, but they will earn an incredible amount of money, or they can have a satisfying job in a field they like, but they will just earn enough money to live modestly.
2. Ask students to choose between the two options, evaluating them based on their knowledge of themselves and their experience.
3. Put students in small groups to share their opinions, including their knowledge and experiences they used to form their opinion.
4. Call on volunteers to share their opinions and reasons with the class.

Learning Outcome

Use the learning outcome to frame the purpose and relevance of Listenings 1 and 2 and the Critical Q activity of weighing benefits and drawbacks. Ask: *What did you learn from the listenings that prepares you participate in a group discussion evaluating the influence money has on happiness?*

▶ *Listening and Speaking 3, page 177*

Vocabulary Skill: Using the dictionary
(5 minutes)

1. Direct students to read the information and examples silently.
2. Check comprehension: *What is similar about the words* creativity *and* productivity? *What is different about them? Why is it a good idea to use a dictionary to choose a word?*
3. Elicit the parts of the dictionary definitions

A (15 minutes)

1. Tell students to first compare the dictionary definitions of the pairs of words.
2. Have students match the words with their definitions.
3. Put students in pairs to compare their answers.
4. Go over the answers with the class.

Activity A Answers, p. 177
1. b, financial; a, economical;
2. a, fun; c, amusement;
3. c, sudden; b, immediate

▶ *Listening and Speaking 3, page 178*

B (5 minutes)

1. Keep students in pairs, but have students complete the sentences individually.
2. Have students compare their answers with their partner. Call on volunteers to read their answers. Elicit or provide corrections as necessary.

Activity B Answers, p. 178
1. economical;   2. financial;   3. immediate;
4. happiness;   5. sudden;   6. fun

C (10 minutes)

1. Keep students in pairs, but have students write their sentences individually.
2. Have students read their sentences aloud to their partner. Call on volunteers to read their sentences.

Activity C Answers, p. 178
Students' answers will vary.

 For additional practice with dictionary definitions, have students visit *Q Online Practice.*

▶ *Listening and Speaking 3, page 179*

SPEAKING

Grammar: Types of sentences (10 minutes)

1. Ask students to silently read the information on types of sentences and the examples.
2. Check comprehension by asking questions: *What are the four types of sentences? Can you give an original example of each type of sentence?*
3. Ask students to silently read the information on punctuation at the end of sentences.
4. Check comprehension by asking questions: *What types of sentences end with a period? What type ends with a question mark? What type ends with an exclamation mark?*

Skill Note

Point out that it is important to know the different types of sentences because, as students will see in the next section, each type has its own intonation.

A (10 minutes)

1. Tell students to read the conversation. Elicit any questions or difficulties.
2. Ask students to identify the sentences individually.
3. Put students in pairs to check their sentences and practice the conversation.

   Activity A Answers, p. 179
   1. exclamatory; **2.** declarative; **3.** declarative;
   4. declarative; **5.** interrogative; **6.** declarative;
   7. declarative; **8.** exclamatory or imperative

▶ *Listening and Speaking 3, page 180*

B (10 minutes)

1. Keep students in pairs. Ask students to quickly read the situations. Elicit any questions or difficulties in vocabulary.
2. Tell students to choose one situation and write a short conversation. Remind them to include a variety of sentence types.
3. Have pairs practice their conversations. Call on volunteers to perform for the class.

   Activity B Answers, p. 180
   Answers will vary.

 For additional practice with sentence types, have students visit *Q Online Practice*.

Pronunciation: Intonation in different types of sentences (10 minutes)

1. Tell students to read the information and examples on intonation in different sentence types.
2. Check comprehension. Ask: *How many sentence types are there?* (4) *How many intonation types are there?* (3) *Which two sentence types have the same intonation?* (declarative and imperative)
3. Ensure that students understand the falling and rising intonation by using your finger to demonstrate.
4. Ask for volunteers to read the sentences. Ask the rest of the class to run their fingers along the arrows as they follow along.

▶ *Listening and Speaking 3, page 181*

A (5 minutes)
CD3, Track 20

1. Tell students they are going to hear a pair of sentences. Tell them to check the type of sentence they hear based on the intonation.

2. Play the audio while students check their answers.
3. Call on volunteers to share their answers.

   Activity A Answers, p. 181
   1. a. yes/no question, b. statement;
   2. a. command, b. *wh-* question;
   3. a. statement, b. exclamation

B (5 minutes)
CD3, Track 21

1. Tell students they are going to listen again and repeat the sentences using the same intonation they hear.
2. Play the audio, pausing for students to repeat.

 For additional practice of intonation, have students visit *Q Online Practice*.

Speaking Skill: Agreeing and disagreeing (5 minutes)

1. Direct students to read the information and phrases about agreeing and disagreeing.
2. Check comprehension: *What are examples of formal ways to agree and disagree? Informal ways?*

21ST CENTURY SKILLS

Group communication can be a challenge when group members don't have the same information. By practicing activities that raise awareness about how to convey and request information, students will be better able to communicate successfully in groups. Help students to develop these skills by conducting group communication activities. Put students in small groups. Ask them to select a leader. Find a simple picture or create a drawing of some geometrical patterns. Give this to the leader. Give a blank sheet of paper to each of the other group members. Explain that the leaders must sit with their backs to their group so that the others can't see the picture. The leaders have to explain the picture to their group in such a way that the group members should be able to draw it on their papers. Tell the group members that they should reproduce whatever their leader tells them to. Give groups 10 minutes to do the activity. Have the groups share their drawings. Tell the groups to discuss how the leader could have given better information and how the group members could have asked for better information.

▶ *Listening and Speaking 3, page 182*

A (10 minutes)

CD3, Track 22

1. Tell students to quickly read the conversation. Elicit any questions or difficulties.

2. Play the audio while students complete the conversation.

3. Check the answers as a class.

4. Put students in pairs to practice the conversation.

> **Activity A Answers, p. 182**
> **1.** That's a good point.   **2.** You can say that again!
> **3.** I don't feel the same way.   **4.** I disagree.

 For additional practice on agreeing and disagreeing, have students visit *Q Online Practice.*

Expansion Activity: Agreeing and disagreeing in different situations (10 minutes)

1. Put students in pairs.

2. Have the pairs think about two different scenarios in which they might agree or disagree with someone. One situation should be a formal situation, such as a conversation in the workplace. The other situation should be an informal situation, such as a conversation between family members.

3. Have the pairs role-play each situation using the appropriate phrases from the Speaking Skill box on page 181.

4. Ask volunteers to perform their conversations for the class.

Unit Assignment:
Take part in a group discussion

Unit Question (5 minutes)

Refer students to the ideas they discussed at the beginning of the unit about whether money can buy happiness. Cue students if necessary by asking specific questions about the content of the unit: *Can sudden wealth make people unhappy? Can happiness lead to more wealth? Why or why not?*

Learning Outcome

1. Tie the unit assignment to the unit learning outcome. Say: *The outcome for this unit is to participate in a group discussion about whether money can buy happiness. This unit assignment is going to let you show your skill in participating in a group*

discussion. *Participating in a group discussion is a useful skill because it allows you to exchange ideas. In doing so, we have the opportunity to learn from and education others.*

2. Explain that you are going to use a rubric similar to their Self-Assessment checklist on page 184 to grade their unit assignment.

Consider the Ideas (5 minutes)

1. Ask students to read the questions. Elicit any questions or difficulties.

2. Put students in pairs to discuss the questions. Remind them to focus on correct intonation as much as they can without sacrificing the content of their discussion.

3. Monitor the discussions, paying attention to students' intonation.

▶ *Listening and Speaking 3, page 183*

Prepare and Speak

Gather Ideas

A (10 minutes)

1. Tell students to reflect on their discussions with their partners. Tell them to write notes about what they can remember.

2. Point out that students should use the questions in the book to guide them. Tell them to write their notes in the book.

Tip for Success (1 minute)

1. Read the tip aloud.

2. Point out that disagreeing is naturally difficult for nearly everyone and typically requires sensitivity. This is one reason why there are formal phrases for disagreeing.

3. Point out that the polite phrases *I know what you mean but...* and *I see your point, but...* can be used in formal and informal situations.

Organize Ideas

B (10 minutes)

1. Tell students to choose one of the questions from the Consider the Ideas activity to discuss.

2. Ask students to use the outline in their books to help them prepare for a group discussion. Remind them not to write exactly what they are going to say and to just write notes to help them organize their ideas.

3. Put students in groups according to the question they would like to discuss. If many students have chosen the same question, form more than one group for that question.

▶ *Listening and Speaking 3, page 184*

Speak

C (10–15 minutes)

1. Review the checklist on page 184. Ask students to read it. Elicit any questions.

2. Depending on the size of your class, you may wish to put students in groups to give their presentation or have students present to the entire class.

3. Remind students not to read directly from their outlines. Remind them to use appropriate intonation according to sentence types, as well as appropriate phrases for agreeing and disagreeing.

4. Use the unit assignment rubric on page 97 of this *Teacher's Handbook* to score each student's presentation.

5. Monitor students' performance as they present.

Alternative Unit Assignments

Assign or have students choose one of these assignments to do instead of, or in addition to, the unit assignment.

1. In this unit, you have heard about factors that influence the effects money can have on our happiness. Brainstorm ways money or wealth can be used so that it will contribute to happiness, rather than create problems. If necessary, do research online to get more ideas. Then form a group, and tell your classmates about your ideas.

2. Think of someone who had to make a choice between having money and being happy. What did they do? How did their choice affect their life? Tell a partner or a group.

 For an additional unit assignment, have students visit *Q Online Practice*.

Check and Reflect

Check

A (5 minutes)

1. Direct students to read and complete the Self-Assessment checklist.

2. Ask for a show of hands for how many students gave all or mostly yes answers.

3. Congratulate them on their success. Discuss the steps they can take if an item on the checklist was difficult for them. For example, if they had trouble with intonation, they can record themselves speaking and ask another student to listen to them.

Reflect

B (5 minutes)

Refer students to the learning outcome on page 165. Tell them to talk with their partners about whether they achieved the learning outcome. Elicit the answers to the unit question that students came up with at the beginning of class. Encourage them to flip through the unit as they discuss the new things they learned and new answers they may have to the unit question.

▶ *Listening and Speaking 3, page 185*

Track Your Success

1. Have students circle the words they have learned in this unit. Suggest that students go back through the unit to review any words they have forgotten.

2. Have students check the skills they have mastered. If students need more practice to feel confident about their proficiency in a skill, point out the page numbers and encourage them to review.

3. Read the learning outcome aloud. Ask students if they feel that they have met the outcome.

Unit 9   Money

Unit Assignment Rubric

Student name: _____

Date: _____

Unit Assignment: *Take part in a group discussion.*

20 = Presentation element was completely successful (at least 90% of the time).
15 = Presentation element was mostly successful (at least 70% of the time).
10 = Presentation element was partially successful (at least 50% of the time).
 0 = Presentation element was not successful.

Take part in a group discussion	20 points	15 points	10 points	0 points
In the group discussion, student spoke easily (without long pauses or reading) when evaluating the influence money has on happiness and was easy to understand (spoke clearly and at a good speed).				
Student used correct signposting.				
Student used intonation correctly according to sentence type.				
Student used vocabulary from the unit.				
Student used appropriate expressions for agreeing and disagreeing, including polite phrases.				

Total points: _____

Comments:

Unit QUESTION
Do we need technology to communicate long distance?

Keeping in Touch

LISTENING • recognizing and understanding definitions
VOCABULARY • idioms
GRAMMAR • comparatives
PRONUNCIATION • unstressed connecting words
SPEAKING • expressing emotions

LEARNING OUTCOME

Role-play a phone call discussing an emotional event you have experienced.

▶ *Listening and Speaking 3, pages 186–187*
Preview the Unit

Learning Outcome

1. Ask for a volunteer to read the unit skills and then the unit learning outcome.

2. Explain: *The learning outcome is what you are expected to be able to do by the unit's end. You are going to be evaluated on how well you meet this outcome. With this in mind, you should focus on learning skills (Listening, Vocabulary, Grammar, Pronunciation, Speaking) that will support your goal of role-playing a phone call to discuss an emotional event you have experienced. This can also help you act as mentors in the classroom to help the other students meet this outcome.*

A (10 minutes)

1. Prepare students for thinking about the topic by having a class discussion about all the reasons why we need to contact others. Start the discussion by asking questions such as: *Why do we contact others? Name some personal reasons. Name some professional reasons.* Write students' opinions on the board. Accept all answers.

2. Put students in pairs or small groups to discuss the first three questions.

3. Call on volunteers to share their ideas with the class. Ask questions to facilitate the discussion: *What do you do if you do not have access to your regular methods of communication? Is communication with some people more important than others? Why?*

4. Focus students' attention on the photo. Have a volunteer describe the photo to the class. Read the questions aloud.

Activity A Answers, p. 187

1. Possible answers: email, cell phone, letters, texting. Reasons may include cost, ease of use, and convenience.
2. The method of communication may depend on how comfortable the other person is with a particular technology, the availability of technology, etc.
3. Students will probably not think this is an effective way to communicate since it reaches people in the local area only.

B (15 minutes)

1. Introduce the Unit Question, "Do we need technology to communicate long distance?" Ask related information questions about personal experience to help students prepare for answering the Unit Question, which is more abstract. *How far away are the people that you communicate with on a regular basis? What would you do if you couldn't use your current method of communication to communicate with them? Have you ever changed the way that you communicate with these people? Why?*

2. Read the Unit Question aloud. Give students a minute to silently consider their answer to the question. Ask students who would answer *yes* to stand on one side of the room and students who would answer *no* to stand on the other side of the room.

3. Direct students to tell a partner next to them their reasons for choosing that side of the issue.

4. Call on volunteers from each side to share their opinions with the class.

5. After students have shared their opinions, provide an opportunity for anyone who would like to change sides to do so.

6. Ask students to sit down, copy the Unit Question and make a note of their answers and reasons. They will refer to these notes at the end of the unit.

Activity B Answers, p. 187
Possible answers: We absolutely need technology to communicate long distance. It is costly to rely on traditional technologies like landline phones, and it takes too long to use traditional mail; It is expensive and slow to use traditional technologies. Regular phones are very expensive and mail takes a long time.

The Q Classroom
CD3, Track 23

1. Play *The Q Classroom*. Use the example from the audio to help students continue the conversation. Ask: *How do some of the students use the computer to communicate long distance? What did some of the students do before we had computer technology? Why do the students think someone might write a letter to communicate long distance?*

▶ *Listening and Speaking 3, page 188*
C (10 minutes)

1. Tell students they are going to complete a chart about methods of communication. Ask students to read the chart. Elicit any questions about vocabulary.

2. Explain that students should think about the advantages and disadvantages of each method and then write them in the correct column.

3. Have students complete the chart individually.

Activity C Answers, p 188

Method	Advantages	Disadvantages
Body language or gestures	You can use it anywhere.	It can be misunderstood. It can only be used face-to-face.
Talking on the telephone	You can speak naturally, and make your meaning clear.	It's not always convenient.
Writing emails	It's easier than writing a letter.	You need to have a computer.

Writing letters	It's nice to have a handwritten letter to keep.	It's slow and you need paper, envelopes, and stamps.
Texting	It's very quick and you can do it on your phone.	Sometimes the number of characters is limited.
Using social networking sites	You can meet other people.	It's not always private.

D (10 minutes)

1. Put students in groups to discuss their choices.

2. Remind them to use reasons and examples to support their opinions.

3. Call on volunteers to report their group's opinions and reasons for them.

Expansion Activity: Different ways for different people (10 minutes)

1. Keep students in their groups from Activity D.

2. Ask students to think about the different ways that they communicate with others. Do they communicate specific ways with specific people? For instance, a student may communicate with her mother mostly by telephone but communicate with her friends mostly by texting.

3. Have students discuss their answers with their groups.

LISTENING

▶ *Listening and Speaking 3, page 189*
LISTENING 1: An Unusual Language

VOCABULARY (15 minutes)

1. Ask students to locate the bold words in each sentence. Pronounce and have students repeat the words.

2. Have students read the sentences and choose the correct answer for each.

3. Call on volunteers to read the answers aloud.

Vocabulary Answers, p. 189
1. a; **2.** a; **3.** c; **4.** b; **5.** c;
6. b; **7.** a; **8.** a; **9.** a; **10.** c

 For additional practice with the vocabulary, have students visit *Q Online Practice*.

 Listening and Speaking 3, page 190

PREVIEW LISTENING 1 (5 minutes)

Direct students to read the information and look at the photo. Ask: *How do you think Silbo might be different from other languages?* (It appears that the hands and fingers are used in forming the sounds, which is unlike most other languages.)

Listening 1 Background Note

Silbo is a whistled language that is also known as Silbo Gomera, or Gomeran Whistle. Silbo is spoken by the inhabitants of La Gomera in the Canary Islands. The island's landscape is full of valleys and deep ravines, making Silbo very effective for communication.

LISTEN FOR MAIN IDEAS (5 minutes)

CD3, Track 24

1. Explain that students are going to listen to the lecture and circle the answer that best completes each statement.

2. Ask students to read the statements. Elicit any questions or difficulties about them.

3. Play the audio and have students circle their answers individually.

4. Elicit the answers from the class.

Main Idea Answers, p. 190
1. c; **2.** a; **3.** b; **4.** c; **5.** a

Tip for Success

Read the tip aloud. Remind students that talks sometimes begin with a question that indicates the speaker's main topic. Point out that speakers may also use questions to signal a change in topic. The questions serve as an introduction to the new content or part of the talk.

 Listening and Speaking 3, page 191

LISTEN FOR DETAILS (10 minutes)

CD3, Track 25

1. Explain that students are going to listen to the lecture again and check the characteristics of Silbo that they hear.

2. Ask students to read the statements. Elicit any questions or difficulties about them.

3. Play the audio and have students check their answers individually.

4. Elicit the answers from the class.

Listen for Details Answers, p. 191
Checked items: 2, 5, 6, 7

 For additional practice with listening comprehension, have students visit *Q Online Practice*.

Listening and Speaking 3, page 192

WHAT DO YOU THINK? (10 minutes)

1. Ask students to read the questions and reflect on their answers.

2. Seat students in small groups and assign roles: a group leader to make sure everyone contributes, a note-taker to record the group's ideas, a reporter to share the group's ideas with the class, and a timekeeper to watch the clock.

3. Give students five minutes to discuss the questions. Call time if conversations are winding down. Allow them an extra minute or two if necessary.

4. Call on each group's reporter to share ideas with the class.

What Do You Think? Answers, p. 192
Answers will vary.
1. Yes, because they are an important part of peoples' culture; No, because very few people speak them and they aren't useful.
2. There is probably a limit to how much you can say.
3. Some advantages include being able to speak with more people and gaining a better understanding of languages in general.

Learning Outcome

Use the learning outcome to frame the purpose and relevance of Listening 1. Ask: *What did you learn from Listening 1 that prepares you to role-play an emotional event you have experienced?*

Listening Skill: Recognizing and understanding definitions (15 minutes)

CD3, Track 26

1. Ask students to read the information about recognizing and understanding definitions. Elicit any difficulties or questions.
2. Check comprehension by asking questions: *What two things should you listen for when you hear an unfamiliar word? Why is it important to be able to recognize when a speaker is going to give a definition?*
3. Tell students to follow along in their books while they listen to the excerpt from Listening 1.
4. Ask students to read the words and phrases used to introduce definition.
5. Check comprehension by asking questions: *What phrase is used to introduce the definition of* hard-wired? *Which phrase is used to introduce the definition of* proliferation?

▶ *Listening and Speaking 3, page 193*

A (15 minutes)

CD3, Track 27

1. Tell students they are going to listen to four sentences and write the definitions they hear.
2. Play the audio while students write the definitions individually. Pause as necessary to give students enough time to write.
3. Put students in pairs to check their answers. Check the answers as a class.

Activity A Answers, p. 193
1. system of sounds;   2. hand movement;
3. rules for forming grammatical sentences;
4. system of writing for the blind or visually impaired that is made with raised dots

B (10 minutes)

1. Tell students that they are going to choose three vocabulary words from the Listening 1 vocabulary on pages 189–190 to write a definition for. Point out that they should include a phrase to introduce the definition.
2. Review the example with the class. Identify the word that is defined in the sentence (*interpret*). Elicit the word that signals the definition (*or*). Point out that the commas are the way that the pause is visually represented to the reader or speaker.
3. Have students write their definitions individually. Walk around and help student as necessary. Do not check answers yet.

Activity B Answers, p. 193
Answers will vary.

C (10 minutes)

1. Put students in pairs to take turns reading their sentences and confirming the definitions.
2. Call on a pair of students to model the example. Remind the student reading the first sentence to pause to signal that a definition is being introduced.
3. Have students ask do the activity. Then call on volunteers to read their sentences to the class. Elicit the definition and the phrase that introduced it.

 For additional practice with recognizing and understanding definitions, have students visit *Q Online Practice.*

▶ *Listening and Speaking 3, page 194*

LISTENING 2: Message in a Bottle

VOCABULARY (15 minutes)

1. Pronounce the words in bold and have students repeat them.
2. Ask students to read the definitions below the paragraphs. Elicit any questions or difficulties.
3. Review the part of speech designations next to each word. Elicit that an idiom is figurative language. Elicit the meaning of figurative language (language that is not used in a literal way).
4. Ask students to read the paragraphs silently. Elicit any questions or difficulties.

5. Tell students to write the words in bold next to the phrase with the correct definition.

6. Put students in small groups to compare their answers. Call on volunteers to share their answers with the class.

> **Vocabulary Answers, p. 194**
> **1.** pen pal; **2.** ancient; **3.** sympathy;
> **4.** out of the blue; **5.** built up; **6.** observe;
> **7.** sealed; **8.** assistance; **9.** one-sided;
> **10.** fighting an uphill battle

MULTILEVEL OPTION

Group lower-level students and assist them with the task. Point out the cues in the words that will help them to understand the word's meaning, for example **fighting an uphill battle** is obviously an idiom. Direct students to read the definitions that are designated idioms. Help them determine synonyms in the idiom and in the definition, e.g., fighting and struggling. Give lower-level students additional sentences to help them determine meaning:

1. According to my mother, trying to keep my 14-year-old brother's room clean is **fighting an uphill battle.**

2. I was watching my favorite show when, **out of the blue,** our TV broke.

Have higher-level students complete the activity individually and then compare answers with a partner. Tell the pairs to write a sentence for each word. Have volunteers write one of their sentences on the board. Correct the sentences with the whole class, focusing on the use of the vocabulary word rather than other grammatical issues.

 For additional practice with the vocabulary, have students visit *Q Online Practice.*

▶ *Listening and Speaking 3, page 195*

PREVIEW LISTENING 2 (5 minutes)

1. Direct students to read the information and look at the photo. Ask: *How do you think the children communicate with each other?*

2. Ask students to check the ways they think the children stay in touch. Point out that they can check more than one. Tell them to check their answers after they listen.

Preview Listening 2 Answer, p. 195
Students' answers will vary. In the listening, the children stay in touch via letters and the unusual method of putting messages in bottles and then putting them in the ocean.

Listening 2 Background Note

The ancient Greek philosopher Theophrastus is the first known person to have put a message in a bottle. He released his bottled message around 310 BC as an experiment to show that the inflowing Atlantic Ocean is what formed the Mediterranean Sea.

Messages in bottles have also been used to signal for help. For example, in May 2005, a group of 88 people who had been shipwrecked off the coast of Costa Rica sent out a cry for help in a message in a bottle. Their message was discovered and they were rescued.

LISTEN FOR MAIN IDEAS (10 minutes)

 CD3, Track 28

1. Tell students they are going to listen to the report about how the children in two different schools communicate. Explain that they should indicate whether the sentences are *T* or *F*.

2. Ask students to read the sentences. Elicit any difficulties with vocabulary or concepts.

3. Play the audio while students work individually.

4. Call on volunteers to share their answers.

> **Listen for Main Idea Answers, p. 195**
> **1.** T; **2.** F; **3.** T; **4.** F; **5.** T

LISTEN FOR DETAILS (5 minutes)

CD3, Track 29

1. Tell students they are going to listen again and circle the correct answer to each question.

2. Ask students to read the questions and answer choices. Elicit any questions or difficulties.

3. Play the audio while students do the activity individually.

4. Go over the answers with the class.

> **Listen for Details Answers, p. 195**
> **1.** c; **2.** b; **3.** a; **4.** b; **5.** b

 For additional practice with listening comprehension, have students visit *Q Online Practice.*

ⓠ WHAT DO YOU THINK?

A (10 minutes)

1. Ask students to read the questions and reflect on their answers.

2. Seat students in small groups and assign roles: a group leader to make sure everyone contributes, a note-taker to record the group's ideas, a reporter to share the group's ideas with the class, and a timekeeper to watch the clock.

3. Give students five minutes to discuss the questions. Call time if conversations are winding down. Allow them an extra minute or two if necessary.

4. Call on each group's reporter to share ideas with the class.

> **Activity A Answers, p. 196**
> Students' answers will vary.
> **1.** People don't know where the bottles will end up or if people will receive them, which makes it interesting.
> **2.** Students may have had pen pals in class or on their own.

B (10 minutes)

1. Have students continue working their small groups to discuss the questions in Activity B. Tell them to choose a new leader, recorder, reporter, and timekeeper.

2. For question 1, recap the main points from the listening. Ask: *What is Silbo? Why is this type of language suitable for the island?*

3. Call on the new reporter to share the group's answers to the questions.

> **Activity B Answers, p. 196**
> Possible answers:
> **1.** These methods of communication developed because they were effective means of communicating.
> **2.** Email and social networking sites have made communication faster and in the case of social networking, more public.

Learning Outcome

Use the learning outcome to frame the purpose and relevance of Listenings 1 and 2 that prepares them for the role-play. Ask: *What did you learn from the listenings that prepares you to role-play a phone call? What did you learn that will help you to define content for your role-play?*

Vocabulary Skill: Idioms (5 minutes)

1. Direct students to read the information and examples silently.

2. Check comprehension: *Are idioms figurative or literal language? What are the two idioms presented? What do they mean? What is the origin of the idiom out of the blue? What is the origin of is a snap? Why is it important to understand and use idioms?*

A (10 minutes)

1. Ask students to read the directions, the sentences and definitions silently. Elicit any questions or difficulties.

2. Put students in pairs to read the sentences and match the idioms with their definitions.

3. Call on volunteers to share their answers.

> **Activity A Answers, p. 197**
> **1.** e; **2.** d; **3.** b; **4.** c; **5.** a

> **MULTILEVEL OPTION**
>
> Group lower-level students and assist them with the task. Help them to find parts of the idiom that relate to their meanings. For example **all ears** contains the word *ears*, which are used for listening. *Ears* are related to the concept of listening in the definition *listening carefully*.
>
> Have higher-level students work in small groups to write a new sentence for idiom. Review them as a class, focusing on whether the idiom is appropriate in the sentence.

Tip for Success

Have students read the tip aloud. Elicit some idioms students may already know. If students are unable to provide any, suggest some simple ones, for example, *on the run* (in a hurry) or *cut to the chase* (leave out the unnecessary details).

B (15 minutes)

1. Keep students in pairs, but have students complete the sentences individually.

2. Have students compare their answers with their partner. Call on volunteers to read their answers.

3. Have pairs practice the conversations.

▶ *Listening and Speaking 3, page 199*

SPEAKING

Grammar: Comparatives (15 minutes)

1. Ask students to silently read the information on comparatives and the examples.

2. Check comprehension by asking questions: *Why do we use comparatives? When do we use -er instead of more than? When do we use as...as? When do we use less than instead of not as ... as?*

3. To make this information clear for students, write the following adjectives on the board: *fast* and *efficient*. Elicit how to make a comparative with each.

   fast → faster, as fast as, not as fast as

   efficient → more efficient, as efficient as, less efficient, not as efficient as

4. Ask students to read the information on irregular adjective forms again. Point out that these adjectives can also be used with *as... as* and *not as... as*. For example, *not as good as, as bad as*, etc.

Skill Note

Have students read the note aloud. Point out that it is important to understand and use comparatives correctly since comparing two things, ideas, or people is very common. It's also helpful when discussing emotion because we tend to think in extremes when we're upset.

▶ *Listening and Speaking 3, page 200*

A (15 minutes)

1. Tell students they are going to use the words and adjectives in parentheses to write two sentences with the same meaning.

2. Review the example with the class. Elicit the comparative structures used in each sentence (*not as...as* and *more than*). Elicit that these sentences are true.

3. Ask students to write their sentences individually. Point out that they should create their own comparison for number 4. Put students in pairs to check their answers.

4. Call on volunteers to share their answers. Accept all answers that can be supported.

B (10 minutes)

1. Keep students in pairs. Ask students to quickly read the situations and example. Elicit any questions or difficulties in vocabulary.

2. Have students tell their partner which method of communication they would use in each situation and why. Remind them to use a comparative instead of simply saying the method of communication.

3. Have pairs discuss their answers. Call on volunteers to share their opinions with the class.

 For additional practice with comparatives, have students visit *Q Online Practice*.

▶ *Listening and Speaking 3, page 201*

Pronunciation: Unstressed connecting words (10 minutes)

🔊 CD3, Track 30

1. Tell students that words used to connect ideas are often unstressed. Point out that they are called connecting words.

2. Review the meaning of stress by asking students to identify the stressed word in a sentence. Say: *Cell phones are smaller than regular phones*, stressing the words *cell, smaller*, and *regular*.

3. Elicit that these words were stressed, or were emphasized by a change in volume. Ask students to tell you why these words were stressed (because they carry the main information or meaning of the sentence). Point out that unstressed words are not stressed because they don't carry information.

4. Play the audio while students follow along.

A (10 minutes)

 CD3, Track 31

1. Tell students they are going to listen to the sentences and write the connecting words they hear.

2. Ask students to read the sentences. Elicit any questions or difficulties. Ask students to read the sentences again and predict the words that belong in the blanks.

3. Play the audio while students check their predictions.

4. Check the answers as a class.

> **Activity A Answers, p. 201**
> **1.** than; **2.** and   **3.** as...as;   **4.** that;   **5.** than

B (5 minutes)

CD3, Track 31

1. Tell students they are going to listen again and repeat the sentences. Remind them not to stress the connecting words.

2. Play the audio, pausing for students to repeat.

web For additional practice of unstressed connecting words, have students visit *Q Online Practice*.

▶ *Listening and Speaking 3, page 202*

Tip for Success

Have students read the tip aloud. Elicit the types of sentences and intonation students learned in Unit 9. Point out that the intonation they use can either support or contrast with the words chosen. Explain that in instances where intonation differs from the words chosen, the intonation will send a stronger message.

Speaking Skill: Expressing emotions
(10 minutes)

1. Direct students to read the information and phrases for expressing emotions.

2. Check comprehension: *What are some phrases to express approval? What are some phrases to express sympathy? Interest? Anger?*

3. Demonstrate how these emotions might sound by reading the specific phrases for each category with that emotion. Elicit which emotion you are conveying.

A (15 minutes)

CD3, Track 33

1. Tell students they are going to listen to and complete a conversation. Ask them to quickly read the conversation. Elicit any questions or difficulties.

2. Play the audio while students complete the conversation. Pause as necessary to give students time to write.

3. Check the answers as a class.

4. Play the conversation again so that students can listen for the emotions.

5. Elicit students' opinions about the emotion of the speakers throughout the conversation (*Emotions range from surprise to anger to surprise to happiness*).

> **Activity A Answers, p. 202**
> **1.** You're kidding!   **2.** I'm fed up with
> **3.** Really?   **4.** That's terrific!

▶ *Listening and Speaking 3, page 203*

B (15 minutes)

1. Tell students they are going to create a conversation to practice expressing emotions. Ask students to quickly read the situations. Elicit any questions or difficulties.

2. Put students in pairs and have them choose one of the situations to create a conversation around.

3. Remind students to think of how to express emotions using the phrases on page 202.

4. Call on volunteers to perform the conversations while the class identifies the emotions and the phrases that express them.

 For additional practice on expressing emotions, have students visit *Q Online Practice*.

Unit Assignment: Role-play a phone call

Unit Question (5 minutes)

Refer students to the ideas they discussed at the beginning of the unit about whether we need technology to communicate long distance. Cue students if necessary by asking specific questions about the content of the unit: *What are some ways people can communicate long distance? What are some unusual ways people communicate long distance? What are some things you prefer to say to someone directly instead of by phone, text, or email?*

Tip for Critical Thinking (1 minute)

Read the tip aloud. Point out role-playing is a common way to practice situations that you may find yourself in later in your academic or professional career. Explain that people often role-play interviews when they are preparing for a job interview or an oral exam.

Critical Q: Expansion Activity

Preparing for a role-play

1. Ask students to think about a job they would like to have in the future, for example, IT specialist, businessperson, manager, etc., and consider the knowledge, skills, and attitudes that this job requires. Tell students to list them.

2. Have students look at their lists and think about how they are ready, or what they may do to become ready for that position.

3. Put students in groups according to the type of job or field that they chose. Tell them to choose a group reporter. Ask students to discuss their lists of knowledge, skills, and attitudes, expanding or refining them as necessary.

4. Call on reporters to share the most common knowledge, skills, and attitudes that their group determined.

5. If time permits, ask students to role-play a job seeker who is making a closing remark about why he or she should be hired for a job.

Learning Outcome

1. Tie the unit assignment to the unit learning outcome. Say: *The outcome for this unit is to role-play a phone call about an emotional event. This unit assignment is going to let you show your skill in role-playing. Role-playing is a useful skill because it allows you to imagine what you would do in a particular situation. In doing so, we have the opportunity to prepare ourselves or reflect on how we present ourselves.*

2. Explain that you are going to use a rubric similar to their Self-Assessment checklist on page 204 to grade their unit assignment.

Consider the Ideas (10 minutes)

1. Ask students to read the statements in the speech bubbles. Elicit any questions or difficulties.

2. Put students in pairs to discuss the statements.

Prepare and Speak

Gather Ideas

A (5 minutes)

Tell students to reflect on recent events that have evoked strong emotions in them. Tell them to list them in their notebooks.

▶ *Listening and Speaking 3, page 204*

Organize Ideas

B (10 minutes)

1. Tell students to choose one of the questions from the consider the ideas activity to role-play.

2. Ask students to write notes to organize their ideas about this event in their books.

Speak

C (10–15 minutes)

1. Review the checklist on page 204. Ask students to read it. Elicit any questions.

2. Put students in pairs to role-play their phone calls.

3. Remind students not to read directly from their outlines. Remind them to express emotions appropriately and use idiomatic language where possible.

4. Use the Unit Assignment Rubric on page 108 of this *Teacher's Handbook* to score each student's presentation.

5. Monitor students' performance as they role-play.

Alternative Unit Assignments

Assign or have students choose one of these assignments to do instead of, or in addition to, the unit assignment.

1. Think about the following life events. What form of communication would you use to tell someone in your family about the event and why? Tell your classmates.

   - You just got a new job.
   - You just lost your job.
   - You had a fight with a close friend.
   - You just inherited a lot of money.

2. Choose an event in the news that recently made you happy, sad, angry, or frightened. Tell a partner about it.

 For an additional unit assignment, please have students visit *Q Online Practice*.

Check and Reflect

Check

A (5 minutes)

1. Direct students to read and complete the Self-Assessment checklist.

2. Ask for a show of hands for how many students gave all or mostly yes answers.

3. Congratulate them on their success. Discuss the steps they can take if an item on the checklist was difficult for them. For example, if they had trouble with expressing emotions, they can record themselves speaking and ask another student to listen to them.

Reflect

B (10 minutes)

1. Refer students to the learning outcome on page 187. Tell them to talk with their partners about whether they achieved the learning outcome.

2. Elicit the answers to the unit question that students came up with at the beginning of class.

3. Encourage them to flip through the unit as they discuss the new things they learned and new answers they may have to the unit question.

▶ *Listening and Speaking 3, page 205*

Track Your Success

1. Have students circle the words they have learned in this unit. Suggest that students go back through the unit to review any words they have forgotten.

2. Have students check the skills they have mastered. If students need more practice to feel confident about their proficiency in a skill, point out the page numbers and encourage them to review.

3. Read the learning outcome aloud. Ask students if they feel that they have met the outcome.

Unit Assignment Rubric

Student name: _____

Date: _____

Unit Assignment: *Role-play a phone call.*

20 = Presentation element was completely successful (at least 90% of the time).
15 = Presentation element was mostly successful (at least 70% of the time).
10 = Presentation element was partially successful (at least 50% of the time).
 0 = Presentation element was not successful.

Role-play a phone call	20 points	15 points	10 points	0 points
Student spoke easily (without long pauses or reading) when expressing an emotional event and was easy to understand (spoke clearly and at a good speed).				
Student expressed emotions appropriately.				
Student did not stress linking words.				
Student used vocabulary from the unit.				
Students used idiomatic language appropriately and correctly where possible.				

Total points: _____

Comments:

Welcome to the Q Testing Program

1. MINIMUM SYSTEM REQUIREMENTS[1]

1024 x 768 screen resolution displaying 32-bit color

Web browser[2]:
Windows®-requires Internet Explorer® 7 or above
Mac®-requires OS X v10.4 and Safari® 2.0 or above
Linux®-requires Mozilla® 1.7 or Firefox® 1.5.0.9 or above

To open and use the customizable tests you must have an application installed that will open and edit .doc files, such as Microsoft® Word® (97 or higher).

To view and print the Print-and-go Tests, you must have an application installed that will open and print .pdf files, such as Adobe® Acrobat® Reader (6.0 or higher).

2. RUNNING THE APPLICATION

Windows®/Mac®
- Ensure that no other applications are running.
- Insert the Q: Skills for Success Testing Program CD-ROM into your CD-ROM drive.
- Double click on the file "start.htm" to start.

Linux®
- Insert the Q: Skills for Success Testing Program CD-ROM into your CD-ROM drive.
- Mount the disk on to the desktop.
- Double click on the CD-ROM icon.
- Right click on the icon for the "start.htm" file and select to "open with Mozilla".

3. TECHNICAL SUPPORT

If you experience any problems with this CD-ROM, please check that your machine matches or exceeds the minimum system requirements in point 1 above and that you are following the steps outlined in point 2 above.

If this does not help, e-mail us with your query at: elt.cdsupport.uk@oup.com
Be sure to provide the following information:

- Operating system (e.g. Windows 2000, Service Pack 4)
- Application used to access content, and version number
- Amount of RAM
- Processor speed
- Description of error or problem
- Actions before error occurred
- Number of times the error has occurred
- Is the error repeatable?

---

[1] The Q Testing Program CD-ROM also plays its audio files in a conventional CD player.

[2] Note that when browsing the CD-ROM in your Web browser, you must have pop-up windows enabled in your Web browser settings.

The Q Testing Program

The disc on the inside back cover of this book contains both ready-made and customizable versions of **Reading and Writing** and **Listening and Speaking** tests. Each of the tests consists of multiple choice, fill-in-the-blanks/sentence completion, error correction, sentence reordering/sentence construction, and matching exercises.

Creating and Using Tests

1. Select "Reading and Writing Tests" or "Listening and Speaking Tests" from the main menu.
2. Select the appropriate unit test or cumulative test (placement, midterm, or final) from the left-hand column.
3. For ready-made tests, select a Print-and-go Test, Answer Key, and Audio Script (for Listening and Speaking tests).
4. To modify tests for your students, select a Customizable Test, Answer Key, and Audio Script (for Listening and Speaking tests). Save the file to your computer and edit the test using Microsoft Word or a compatible word processor.
5. For Listening and Speaking tests, use the audio tracks provided with the tests. **Audio files for the listening and speaking tests can also be played in a standard CD player.**

Reading and Writing Tests

Each test consists of 40 questions taken from the selected unit. The Reading and Writing Tests assess reading skills, vocabulary, vocabulary skills, grammar, and writing skills.

Listening and Speaking Tests

Each test consists of 40 questions taken from the selected unit. The Listening and Speaking Tests assess listening skills, vocabulary, vocabulary skills, grammar, pronunciation, and speaking skills.

Cumulative Tests

The placement tests for both Listening and Speaking and Reading and Writing consist of 50 questions. Each placement test places students in the correct level of *Q*: Introductory–5. **A printable User Guide to help you administer the placement test is included with the placement test files on the CD-ROM.**

The midterm tests for both Listening and Speaking and Reading and Writing consist of 25 questions covering Units 1–5 of the selected Level. The midterm Reading and Listening texts are new and not used in any other tests or student books.

The final tests for both Listening and Speaking and Reading and Writing consist of 25 questions covering Units 6–10 of the selected Level. The final Reading and Listening texts are new and not used in any other tests or student books.